Early Childhood Development in Tonga

WORLD BANK STUDY

Early Childhood Development in Tonga

Baseline Results from the Tongan Early Human Capability Index

Sally Brinkman and Binh Thanh Vu

WORLD BANK GROUP

Contents

Figures

Maps

Photos

Tables

Foreword by Alice Albright and Amit Dar

The World Bank Group's Education Global Practice and the Global Partnership for Education work closely with national governments and development partners to develop education strategies and programs that reflect a deep commitment to achieving education results and creating a favorable climate for investment in education. The overarching aim in the era of the Sustainable Development Goals (SDGs) is to mobilize increased financing to strengthen national education systems that deliver quality education, especially to benefit children from the poorest families. With a vastly more ambitious set of education targets to achieve by 2030, donors and their partners have a more crucial role than ever in leveraging sustainable investments.

The education SDG covers targets spanning every level of education, from preschool to tertiary and beyond. The new focus on early childhood development—covering both education and health—is linked not only to the rights of children to these services but also to the long-term development of their cognitive skills. As studies in Mozambique and Jamaica have shown, children receiving quality early childhood education are better prepared to learn when they enter primary school and to earn higher incomes as adults. This has profound implications for families trying to break the intergenerational transmission of poverty as well as economies trying to raise productivity and skills.

One prerequisite to delivering on the SDG targets is country capacity to monitor service delivery. Good quality data collection systems to monitor child development and early education outcomes are crucial for evidence-based policy and strategic planning. Australia was the first country in the world to develop national census systems to monitor early child development, and standard literacy and numeracy outcomes, in years three, five, and nine. We are very proud that with support from the World Bank and the Global Partnership for Education, Tonga is now the second country in the world to establish a sound monitoring system and to undertake a country-wide census of child development. Our commitment to monitoring systems through population-wide data collections stems from the recognition that governments, stakeholders, schools, and communities need powerful and reliable local data for planning and advocacy.

The Early Human Capability Index developed for Tonga captures multiple aspects of a child's development, providing insights to help shape and improve early childhood services. The results of the Tonga census show that some communities are doing better than others, underscoring the importance of reading and stimulation for children in their early years in the home environment, as well as the importance of receiving early childhood services. Over half of Tonga's children have not yet experienced an early education program, so these baseline findings provide early evidence for continued investments to ensure high quality early child development opportunities for all.

This report not only provides an excellent roadmap for child-friendly policies and programs for Tonga, it also exemplifies a process that can be emulated by other countries, one of true local engagement and ownership, with technical support provided to build local system-wide monitoring capacity.

Through the Pacific Early Age Readiness and Learning (PEARL) Programme, other countries in the Pacific will now be able to follow Tonga's lead. Moreover, the implementation of PEARL in Tonga should provide valuable information on unit costs, so that issues of scalability and sustainability in early-age-readiness programs are fully understood.

We are grateful to all those involved in making the data collection a success, and we particularly congratulate the government of Tonga for its proactive leadership in understanding the importance of early child development and education for the country's future prosperity.

Alice Albright
Chief Executive Officer
Global Partnership for Education

Amit Dar
Acting Director, Education Global Practice
World Bank

Foreword by Ana Maui Taufe'ulungaki

Tonga has been concerned for some time that it was not making satisfactory progress in its educational performance, and that it lacked reliable data on which to assess its performance. The PEARL program was a welcome initiative to provide Tonga with accessible and accurate information on which to base policy and strategic directions in the early years of education.

I was very privileged to have been associated with this groundbreaking work, in expectation that the PEARL program to ensure that all children in Tonga, irrespective of their socioeconomic status and location, would have access to early childhood education and come to school ready to learn. Based on the survey information, curriculum materials and teaching and learning strategies would be developed that are relevant and appropriate for Tonga's educational context and would meet the needs of all Tongan children.

Tonga has high expectations of the outcomes of the PEARL program, and that it will benefit all children in Tonga.

Dr. Ana Maui Taufe'ulungaki
Former Minister of Education and Training, Tonga

Acknowledgments

This report was funded through the Global Partnership for Education. The development of the Tongan Early Human Capability Index (TeHCI) was led by Dr. Sally Brinkman in consultation with Kakatisi Taulava (early childhood education officer, Ministry of Education and Training); Soana Kitiona (early childhood education officer, Ministry of Education and Training); Alison Tu'ionetoa (former senior officer for early childhood education schools, Wesleyan Schools Office); Amelia Tu'ionetoa (former principal, Maamaloa Preschool); Monalisa Tukuafu (president, Tonga Preschool Association); Soane Vahe (director, Catholic Education System); Alisi Fifita (senior public health sister, Ministry of Health); Nadia Fifita (director, Ocean of Light International School); and many others who participated in the development and implementation process. The finalization of the TeHCI instrument was done with strong support from all concerned ministries, district officers, and town officers.

The data collection was undertaken through a memorandum of understanding between the Ministry of Health and the Ministry of Education and Training. The development of the memorandum was significantly facilitated by Sela Paasi (Director of Nursing, Ministry of Health) and Dr. Toakase Fakakovikaetau (community pediatrician).

The authors acknowledge the work of the district community health nurses and early childhood teachers who collected the TeHCI data across Tonga, and those who helped with the data entry. Sincere thanks go to Soana Kitiona (early childhood education officer, Ministry of Education and Training), who managed the pilot data collection and worked with Dr. Brinkman through all the translations and back translation of the TeHCI instrumentation. Special thanks go to Siosi Tapueluelu (PEARL coordinator, World Bank) who managed the TeHCI data collection across Tonga. The data collection would not have been as successful without Siosi's dedication to detail and expert management and project coordination skills.

Special appreciation goes to Richard Atelea Kautoke (senior Geographical Information Systems specialist and head of the Lands and Geographic Information Systems Unit, Ministry of Lands, Survey and Natural Resources) and his team for the geographical mapping of the TeHCI data. The mapped data was crucial for making its visual dissemination easily accessible to communities. Thanks also go to Ata'ata Finau' (government statistician, Statistics Department) for providing detailed population data from the 2011 Tongan Census for the estimated denominator data.

The authors also thank key people within the Ministry of Education and Training, namely Dr. Raelyn 'Esau (deputy chief executive officer, Policy and Planning); Oketi Akau'ola (chief education officer, Teaching and Learning Division); and Emily Pouvalu (chief executive officer, Ministry of Education and Training). The authors sincerely thank the Minister of Education and Training, Dr. Ana Maui Taufe'ulungaki, for her commitment to early childhood education initiatives in Tonga, and her active support of the PEARL program.

The authors thank the peer reviewers Gabriel Pillay and David Coleman (Department of Foreign Affairs and Trade of Australia); Dr. Mary Young (director, Center for Child Development of China Development Research Foundation); and Dr. Sophie Naudeau (senior education specialist, World Bank), who provided valuable comments for improving the report.

From the World Bank team, the authors acknowledge all members of the PEARL team who contributed to the report, and Kris McDonall (program assistant) for significant operational support throughout the project.

About the Authors

Sally Brinkman is an epidemiologist focusing on the effect of societies on child development. She is a co-director of the Fraser Mustard Centre, an initiative of the Telethon Kids Institute; an associate professor at the University of Western Australia; and an adjunct associate professor at the University of Adelaide. Dr. Brinkman works with governments and donor organizations on measures of child development for monitoring and evaluation purposes. She has written more than 100 publications covering child health, development and early education, alcohol-related violence, and teenage pregnancy. She has a master's degree in public health and a PhD in pediatric epidemiology.

Binh Thanh Vu is a senior education specialist in the East Asia and Pacific region at the World Bank. She is based in Sydney, Australia, where she leads the World Bank's education team for Timor-Leste, Papua New Guinea, and the Pacific Islands. Binh has worked for the World Bank for 17 years. Her work in the Pacific is supported by her analytical and operational experience in the East Asia and Pacific region and the Europe and Central Asia region in policy analysis and policy development from early childhood education, and primary-to-higher education. She has worked on analytical reports, on policy and technical notes, and on the design of education operations for quality improvement, including quality education for disadvantaged groups. She has also worked on public expenditure reviews in education, and education planning and budgeting. She has masters degrees in economics as well as in education management and administration.

Abbreviations

EDI	Early Development Instrument
NCD	noncommunicable disease
PEARL	Pacific Early Age Readiness and Learning
PIC	Pacific Island country
SDG	Sustainable Development Goal
TeHCI	Tongan Early Human Capability Index

Executive Summary

Early childhood development is the holistic development of children from conception to about eight years. Development is defined as the process of change in which children come to master increasingly complex levels of moving, thinking, feeling, and interacting with people and objects in their environment. The various aspects of development tend to be called developmental domains.

Recent studies in Tonga show poor reading outcomes in the first three grades of primary education, and little understanding from communities of the importance of the first years of a child's life on development, learning, and later successes. Based on these results as well as other studies and assessments, the Tonga Ministry of Education and Training requested technical assistance from the World Bank to embark on a joint mission to improve the learning outcomes of the country's children.

The Pacific Early Age Readiness and Learning (PEARL) Programme, financed by the Global Partnership for Education and implemented by the World Bank, aims to support Pacific Island countries and their development partners in building capacity to design, implement, and monitor evidence-based integrated policies and programs that prepare children and their families for primary school. PEARL's two focus areas are reflected in its two visions: (1) that all children in the Pacific have access to and benefit from programs in their communities that promote healthy, stimulating, and culturally relevant experiences that prepare them for preprimary, primary schooling, and life; and (2) all classrooms in the early grades of primary education are equipped with the knowledge and the resources to ensure children become literate in a language they are familiar with, and that they are able to use these skills and knowledge to engage in lifelong learning.

Recognizing that to achieve the greatest education impacts it is important to start early, the Ministry of Education and Training and the World Bank developed a tool to measure the capability of Tongan children in the years before they enter primary school, and conducted a census of all three- to five-year-olds in the country. Unlike many child development tools used around the world, the

Tongan Early Human Capability Index (TeHCI) measures the capability of children rather than "developmental delay" or pathology. The positive and negative aspects of how a child is developing are assessed with the TeHCI, which has the potential to place a child on a developmental trajectory rather than simply a bimodal pass/fail outcome. The concept of early human capability is also not limited to a single aspect of development and allows for a holistic approach to child development.

The TeHCI measures development across the most commonly accepted domains, as well as some others that are considered important in Tonga. After consultations with stakeholders in Tonga's early childhood care and education sector, it was agreed to focus on the following domains: physical health, verbal communication, cultural identity and spirituality, social and emotional well-being and skills, perseverance and approaches to learning, numeracy and concepts, and literacy (reading and writing).

The results produced some expected results reflecting global evidence, as well unexpected ones, providing a valuable evidence-base with which to design pilot interventions in communities under the PEARL program. The main findings are:

- *Girls outperform boys.* Across all domains with the exception of approaches to learning, girls show better results than boys for children ages three to five, which is consistent with the global literature.
- *Mother's educational background makes a difference.* In Tonga, children are more likely to do better on all aspects of child development if their primary caregiver has a higher educational background. Mothers with higher educational levels will generally be able to generate greater levels of resources to support their families, and have more taught skills to be able to pass on through everyday stimulation and interaction with their children. The results also showed the mother's educational level is strongly associated with a child's participation in some form of early education program, which also has a positive impact on development.
- *Little or no difference across islands.* With the majority of Tonga's population residing in the main island of Tongatapu, it was expected children would perform better there than in the outer islands that lack access to services to the same extent as Tongatapu. But with the exception of physical development, this trend was not seen.
- *Family interaction with child positively impacts development.* Children have higher literacy levels if they come from households where they are read to; however, higher levels of development can be seen for these children across all the developmental domains. This likely reflects a more interactive and supportive home environment for healthy development. Further analysis also showed a relationship between the likelihood of children having higher levels of interaction and stimulation in the home is related to the mother's educational level, and is most pronounced for reading with the child.

- *Reading with children and preschool positively impact development.* The impact of reading in the home environment is actually larger than that of attending preschool (that is, children who attend preschool but are not read to at home show poorer outcomes than those who are). For children who are not being read to at home, however, the impact of preschool is positive. Participation in some form of early childhood education program has a statistically significant effect on every aspect of development except for verbal skills and perseverance, and was highest for literacy outcomes and numeracy and concepts.

The results from the TeHCI also show that over half of all children in Tonga attend school for the first time without exposure to any early education program, which includes some form of preschool, kindergarten, early education center, or playgroup. International literature suggests these children will find it harder to transition into the school environment, and are at a higher risk of dropping out of school early and failing in school. This indicator is affected by geography, with the remote island group of Ha'apai showing low rates of participation. It is also likely to be influenced by local leadership since most preschool services across Tonga are community-based, thus requiring local leadership and support.

With the assistance of the Mapping Office of the Department of Survey and Lands, the TeHCI results were geographically mapped to provide communities with a clear visual representation of how their children were performing compared to children in other communities on various domains of development. The results were disseminated to all communities across the country through a series of public meetings, provoking discussions that led to the development of a pilot community-based intervention aimed at encouraging parents and caregivers to play and interact with their children to improve school readiness.

CHAPTER 1

Introduction

Context of Tonga

The Kingdom of Tonga is a proud country, having never lost indigenous power or sovereignty to a foreign power. The archipelago is located within the Polynesian region of the Pacific Ocean; it includes 176 islands covering 718 square kilometers, of which 36 islands are inhabited, although some are very remote. The kingdom is divided into five main island groups: Tongatapu, Vava'u, 'Eua, Ha'apai, and the Niuas. The Tongatapu group includes the largest island (Tongatapu) where most (70 percent) of the population live in the capital, Nuku'alofa, which is the main commercial center and harbor. Nuku'alofa is over 2,000 kilometers from its nearest large market, New Zealand, and over 3,000 kilometers from Australia.

Over the last decade, the separation between the government and the monarchy has gradually increased. In 2010, Tonga held its first representative elections, becoming a constitutional monarchy, having previously been an autochthonous monarchy. The Kingdom of Tonga is considered an upper-middle-income economy, and is largely dependent on foreign aid and remittances from Tongans working overseas (primarily in New Zealand and to a lesser extent Australia and the United States). The economy is traditionally redistributive and based on three core values: 'ofa (love), faka'apa'apa (respect), and fatongia (responsibility). Foreign land ownership is prohibited in Tonga, although land can be leased by foreigners. Additionally, land can only be owned by men, with widowed women having to place land titles in their father's or son's names.

Tonga, as with many of the other small Pacific Island countries (PICs), is largely shaped by its economic geography. The population is just over 100,000, and net migration out of Tonga is high, with over 66 percent of the population living abroad. Absolute poverty is low, and development outcomes are relatively strong. Average annual per capita incomes are approximately US$3,200, higher than most of the countries in the Pacific (although still well below some of those islands that are more integrated with metropolitan countries such as American Samoa, Cook Islands, and New Caledonia). The majority of households engage in some form of subsistence food production and handicrafts, and family groups rely on traditional economic cooperation. Most families, particularly on the outer islands are self-sufficient, producing almost all basic food needs from farming and fishing. Strong family and church networks, as well as extensive subsistence agricultural production, means that food poverty is virtually nonexistent.

Even so, Tonga is facing a serious challenge in securing prosperity for all and significant numbers live in hardship. In 2011, the World Bank prepared internationally comparable poverty estimates for Tonga and other Pacific Islands for the first time. These showed the prevalence of extreme poverty is very low in Tonga at 1.1 percent of the population, suggesting there are fewer than 1,200 people living in extreme poverty. Poverty based on the US$3.10-a-day line is somewhat higher, at 8.2 percent of the population, with rural populations more likely to live in poverty than those in urban areas (9.1 percent compared to 4.9 percent). This is consistent with local views that although there are very few people living in abject poverty in Tonga, "hardship"—or lack of cash for basic goods—is significantly more widespread.

Tonga is a small, open economy. It is heavily reliant on imports, which are equivalent to about 40 percent of gross national income, and faces a large structural trade deficit. The country is also heavily reliant on external investment in industries such as tourism. Overseas development assistance has been central to the government's service delivery efforts and is likely to remain so. In this environment, good domestic policies and leadership are necessary but not always sufficient for progress; external factors are crucial to development outcomes.

Unlike many PICs, Tonga performed strongly on most of the Millennium Development Goals. Health indicators have improved steadily, and access to safe water and sanitation is widespread. About 98 percent of Tongan women give birth in the presence of skilled birth attendants. Under-five mortality is 23 per 1,000 live births (the best of any of the World Bank's Pacific Island member countries), and continues to decline steadily. Maternal mortality is low, with an average of two reported deaths per year associated with birth-related complications. Another improving indicator is the proportion of children immunized against measles, reaching 99 percent in 2009 (Ministry of Finance and National Planning 2010). Tonga's immunization program is seen as one of the country's most successful interventions. Such interventions seem to be well accepted at the community level, mostly due to the trust building that child health nurses have been able to establish on the ground. Child health nurses are highly respected in the community and underscore the increasing quality of the national child health system.

The growing crisis of noncommunicable diseases (NCD) threatens to reverse improvements. Some evidence suggests that life expectancy in Tonga has unfortunately been declining because of NCDs (female life expectancy was 72.8 years in 2000 and 70.5 in 2011), with chronic diseases, namely diabetes, on the rise. The latest Global Burden of Disease 2013 study, covering 188 countries, showed the rising importance of NCDs as a cause of global death and disability. NCDs are now the leading cause of death for most countries in the Pacific. Tonga also has the highest obesity rate (58 percent) in the PICs, and much higher than the 13 percent global average (Hou, Anderson, and Burton-Mckenzie 2016).

Tonga is performing very well on the Millennium Development Goal-related targets of student participation in primary education, with 2010 figures showing that 93 percent of children were enrolled and little or no difference between enrollment rates for boys and girls. Of those children who were enrolled in primary school, 90 percent reach the last grade of primary schooling, which runs from ages 6 to 14. While primary school enrollment rates are high, they decline rapidly after age 15, and in 2010 about 15 percent of 16-year-olds were not attending school. School drop out from the secondary system is more marked for boys. As of 2007, the drop-out rate for boys enrolled in government middle and secondary schools was 56 percent, and 58 percent for nongovernment schools. As well as the government, which provides free primary education, churches play a central role in Tonga's education system, particularly at the secondary level. However, the results from a 2014 survey using the Early Grade Reading Assessment revealed that, at the end of grade 1, one in four children did not know the sounds of any letters, and two-thirds had no reading comprehension.

The remoteness, isolation, and small populations of Tonga's 36 inhabited islands present challenges to the design, financing, implementation, monitoring, and evaluation of policies and all services and programs. At the national level, many governments in the Pacific lack the capacity to systematically monitor important outcome measures to track their country's progress. In particular, early childhood units within ministries of education are notorious for being critically understaffed; in Tonga, for example, only two staff were dedicated to early childhood education at the time of the TeHCI survey. Although Tonga's Education Act of 2013 specifically addresses early childhood education and preschool, and thus provides a policy framework to work with, the reality is that—like most governments everywhere—early childhood education is not included in the national budget. In 2012, however, Tonga's government initiated a small grant of T$50 per year per child enrolled in a registered early childhood education center. Without resources and staff, early childhood education units in the Pacific lack the capacity to coordinate and allocate resources to support school readiness. In Tonga, it could be assumed that private and public expenditure for preschool is low, although the total size of investment in preschool is difficult to calculate. However, the 2009 Household Income and Expenditure Survey found fees paid by households for preschool in Tonga amounted to about T$106 per year, including the value of in-kind fees, but parents of only 39 percent of preschool students actually reported paying preschool fees (Andrich, Sheridan, and Luo 2005). Obviously, preschool fees alone underestimate the magnitude of investment in preschool. They do not capture cash or in-kind donations, which are believed to be substantial. Most teaching staff are volunteers or partially remunerated, and the value of their time volunteered represents an economic cost since they could have been engaged in other productive activities. Even so, the total funding for preschool is low, especially given the international evidence for the rate of return for expenditure on preschools. With scant resources, preschooling is limited to those who can afford it, thus excluding many of the poorest children.

The Pacific Early Age Readiness and Learning Programme

The Pacific Early Age Readiness and Learning (PEARL) Programme is funded by the Global Partnerships for Education through the Global and Regional Activities Program. The US$8.5 million program is being executed by the World Bank Education Global Practice, and aims to support PICs and their development partners to build capacity to design, implement, and monitor evidence-based integrated policies and programs that prepare children and their families for primary school. The two focus areas of PEARL are reflected in its two visions: (1) that all young children in the Pacific have access to quality early childhood development and education in their communities, and benefit from programs that promote healthy, stimulating, and culturally relevant experiences that prepare them for preprimary, primary schooling, and life; and (2) all classrooms in the early grades of primary education are equipped with the knowledge and the resources to ensure young children become literate in a language they are familiar with, and are able to use these skills and knowledge to engage in lifelong learning. To this end, PEARL will focus primarily on developing capacity within ministries of education to lead policies and programs in partnership with relevant local stakeholders and private and nongovernment service providers.

The PEARL program's key objectives are:

- To inform policy dialogue on key areas of education investment in the early years of child development through the production of diagnostic analytical work on early childhood care and education services and student learning outcomes, with a focus on school readiness and early grade literacy.
- To identify and pilot evidence-based policy options to improve the efficiency of early child care and education services and early grade literacy, based on global innovations, best practice, and data generated in the diagnostic analyses.
- To build capacity in ministries of education to design pilot interventions in these areas to address national education priorities, as identified by governments and development partners.
- To support greater access to global innovations and best practice to the region's growing community of practice.

PEARL Pillars

The PEARL program has three pillars of activities:

- *Pillar I: Pilot interventions on school readiness and early grade reading.* This includes the implementation of a full cycle of activities, from diagnostic assessment of school readiness and early reading levels to designing and piloting interventions on school readiness and early grade literacy (Tonga PEARL).
- *Pillar II: Regional knowledge generation activities.* This includes discrete pieces of technical assistance and analytical advisory activities to improve the evidence

base of countries to inform short- and medium-term policy agendas, with the aim to increase the school readiness of young children and early grade literacy levels (Tuvalu PEARL, Samoa PEARL, Kiribati PEARL, and Papua New Guinea PEARL; other countries may join in the later stages of PEARL implementation).

- *Pillar III: Regional knowledge exchange events.* This includes a series of regional workshops, training sessions, and conferences, as well as the twinning of government staff across participating PICs to exchange knowledge and experiences at a practical level in school readiness and early grade literacy.

Tonga PEARL

Tonga is the first country the PEARL program started in. The project's overall objective is to support the government's vision for early child care and education, and the development of foundational literacy skills in the early grades. The four specific objectives for this activity are:

- Increasing the participation of young children in early child care and education services beyond formal preschool.
- Broadening family and community perceptions around school readiness and early childhood development.
- Improving early literacy outcomes of children in classes 1–2.
- Establishing the basis of a population-level monitoring and evaluation system on school readiness and early grade literacy that can help the Ministry of Education and Training and development partners inform short- and medium-term policy decisions in these areas.

The school readiness and early grade literacy components of the PEARL program include a mix of processes, community and teacher output, and child/student-level outcomes. To achieve this, the school readiness component will:

- Strengthen multisectoral governance in Tonga to support early child care and education.
- Implement a national monitoring system for school readiness across Tonga that includes the development of the Tongan Early Human Capability Index (TeHCI).
- Pilot sustainable and low-cost interventions in more than 30 percent of communities to increase school readiness of children by (1) increasing parent and community awareness of the importance of preschool and home activities, (2) training and capacity building focusing on areas of weakness identified through the TeHCI baseline, and (3) measuring change in TeHCI results in pilot communities versus nonpilot communities.
- Share outcomes, lessons, and cost data with small countries of the Pacific and donors, together with lessons learned about implementation.

Early Childhood Development in Tonga • http://dx.doi.org/10.1596/978-1-4648-0999-6

The early grade literacy component aims to improve the effectiveness of teaching and learning reading in the early grades. The main outcome of the intervention is the improvement of reading and writing skills of children in classes 1 and 2 (children ages six to seven). Reading and writing interventions were designed based on the findings of a survey using the Tonga Early Grade Reading Assessment.

The intervention is being carried out at the community level for the school readiness component, and at the school and class level for the early grade literacy component. The planned randomized design allocates half of a sample of Tongan communities to receive the school readiness intervention, in which community-appointed volunteers receive training and resources to assist facilitation of community play-based activities. Thirty percent of all communities across Tonga receive this support, although community awareness activities, including monitoring child development, are taking place in all communities. The intention was to select a sample of schools that serve the sample of communities in treatment and control groups, with half allocated to receive the reading intervention. However, 15 schools receiving interventions from two other donor-funded programs—the Literacy and Leadership Initiative and the Pacific School Literacy Support Program—were excluded from the PEARL program's reading intervention.

Table 1.1 shows the schedule and research of Tonga PEARL.

As such, the key intermediate outcome of the PEARL program is to produce a baseline of child development, and determine the magnitude of disparities in child development across the country. The purpose of the data collection was

Table 1.1 Tonga PEARL Schedule and Research

Born in	2013–2014 (baseline)	2015 (year 1)	2016 (year 2)	2017 (year 3)
2013	0 years	1 years	2 years	3 years
2012	1 years	2 years	3 years	4 years
2011	2 years	3 years	4 years	5 years
2010	3 years	4 years	5 years	6 years
2009	4 years	5 years	6 years	7 years
2008	5 years	6 years	7 years	8 years
2007	6 years	7 years	8 years	9 years
2006	7 years	8 years	9 years	10 years

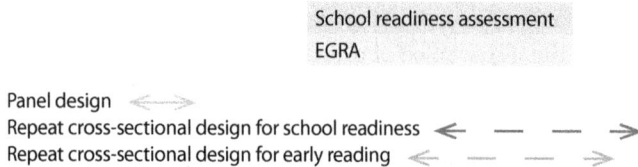

School readiness assessment
EGRA

Panel design
Repeat cross-sectional design for school readiness
Repeat cross-sectional design for early reading

Source: PEARL program description and results framework, February 2014.
Note: EGRA = Early Grade Reading Assessment; PEARL = Pacific Early Age Readiness and Learning.

also to collect information about the learning environment provided in the home—as indicated by the engagement of parents with their children in learning activities such as singing, reading books, telling stories, and playing games—and the reasons for either engaging or not engaging in existing early childhood education services.

CHAPTER 2

The Importance of Measuring Early Childhood Development

Early Childhood Development and School Readiness

Early childhood development is the holistic development of children from conception. Development is defined as the process of change in which children master increasingly complex levels of moving, thinking, feeling, and interacting with people and objects in their environment. The various aspects of development tend to be called developmental domains.

Children develop at different rates on each of the various developmental domains. For example, children generally start to crawl from 6 to 10 months of age. This is considered the normal developmental age range for this ability, and the entire period during which it can appear is considered on course for healthy development. The rates and patterns of development during the early years are highly variable, however, and not all children who are doing well are doing the same thing at the same time. Development is considered to be delayed when children have not reached these developmental milestones within the expected time. For example, if the normal range for learning to walk is between nine and 15 months, and a 20-month-old child has still not begun walking, this would be considered a "developmental delay."

The dimension of early human capability allows for the measurement of both the positive and negative aspects of how a child is developing, as opposed to developmental delay or pathology. The measurement of early human capability has the potential to place a child on a developmental trajectory rather than simply a bimodal pass/fail outcome. The concept of early human capability is also not limited to a single aspect of development and allows for a holistic approach to child development.

Studies investigating early human capability tend to discuss physical health and the cognitive and noncognitive aspects of human development. Physical health from a developmental standpoint generally includes height and weight (for the calculation of stunting and wasting), and indicators of how sickly a child is. Cognitive development includes abstract problem solving skills, and early literacy and numeracy skills, while the noncognitive aspects include a child's social and emotional development, such as self-regulation and temperament, and can also include approaches to learning and perseverance. That said, no single measure of child development that exists today captures each of these aspects of early human capability.

Closely aligned to the concept of early human capability is the concept of school readiness. While early human capability can be measured across a wider age range, school readiness is located at a particular time in a child's life. Depending on local laws and education systems, this generally occurs at about age five. If children are "school ready," then they should be entering the education system with all the skills, capabilities, health, and development to take advantage of the school learning environment. Globally, school readiness is gaining currency as a viable strategy to close the learning gap and improve equity in achieving lifelong learning and full developmental potential among children. School readiness supports the adoption of policies and standards for early learning, expanding the provision of opportunities beyond formal center-based services to target those who are excluded. School readiness is linked with positive social and behavioral competencies in adulthood, as well as improved academic outcomes in primary and secondary school in terms of equity and performance. In addition, school readiness is gaining attention as a strategy for economic development. Approaches to economic growth and development consider human capital as a key conduit for sustained and viable development, the inception of which begins in the early years.

By the simplest definition, children who are ready for school have the basic minimum skills and knowledge in a variety of domains that will enable them to be successful in school. These minimum standards set the bar for what children should know and be able to do, so they enter school ready and eager to learn, thereby enabling a successful transition into a primary school learning environment (Sandraluz and others 2004). Success in school is determined by a range of basic behaviors and abilities, including literacy, numeracy, ability to follow directions, working well with other children, and engaging in learning activities (Brooks-Gunn, Rouse, and McLanahan 2007).

School readiness skills are considered to be cumulative in that there exists a hierarchy of achievement based on mastering earlier goals; that is, children build on earlier learned skills and behaviors. In this sense, readiness combines learning and development because achieving simpler skills allows for the acquisition of higher and more complex skills (Bowman, Donovan, and Burns 2001). Children entering primary school, for example, need a working vocabulary to master reading skills. In other words, learning achievement in school is the product of a process of acquiring skills from birth. Advanced skills build upon the mastery of former skills.

Measuring Early Childhood Development

The enthusiasm to measure child rights, development, and well-being has been facilitated by the United Nations Convention on the Rights of the Child. Until recently, the focus was on the rights of children to be healthy, whereas there is now a move toward a more holistic appreciation of childhood, and for children to have opportunities to develop to their full capacity. The desire to ensure that the maximum number of children reach their full potential as adults is of critical importance to future societies.

At the same time, governments are beginning to understand the importance of developing systems for monitoring and evaluation, which are fundamental to support evidence-based policy, management, and accountability. Access to quality child development data can help identify patterns across populations and inform decision making to achieve positive change for communities requiring support. Countries need to collect relevant and timely child development data to progress in supporting their children. Quick access and more efficient use of such data make it possible to identify education opportunities and challenges, and develop relevant strategies in response.

Healthy child development needs to be reflected through various domains of development: physical, social and emotional, and cognitive. It has been demonstrated that each of these domains can be measured reliably at the time of transition to school. Moreover, these measures can be interpreted as reflecting the complexity of a child's developmental status before starting school, as well as predicting future outcomes. Most importantly, each domain strongly predicts subsequent school success; in other words, it is not just cognitive development that predicts later school success. Indeed, for every aspect of weakness in development, the risk of school failure increases.

The dimension of child development, as opposed to developmental pathology, allows for the measurement of both positive and negative aspects of how a child is developing, as well as allowing for a holistic approach to the child. Child development measures that have the potential to place a child on a developmental trajectory, rather than simply a bimodal pass/fail outcome, are the most useful for country-wide monitoring and evaluation systems.

As reflected in Young (2007), there are many important reasons why governments are recognizing the importance of measuring early childhood development, including:

- *Monitoring the state of early childhood development at the level of the population.* As now ratified by the Convention on the Rights of the Child, countries are required to monitor how well children are developing within and across their populations. Monitoring raises the profile of this issue and is a strong advocacy for children and families, as well as providing a base level of information to mobilize action. With public access to the results of monitoring, civil servants, nongovernment organizations, aid agencies, and the media are able to advocate for children and families, promoting new policy issues to be recognized and addressed.
- *Monitoring early childhood development over time.* This enables communities and populations to determine whether they are making improvements. Only by monitoring over time can policy makers and service providers determine whether their actions are making a difference to the new generations of

children born every year. If improvements are made across societies and population groups to help support families and schools, improvements over successive cohorts of children should—one would hope—be made.

- *Identification of resilience in communities that support child development.* Population measurements (such as a census) of child development enable the relative comparison of communities. Comparing how communities do leads to the question of why some communities do better than others? What are the strengths and weaknesses that help support families, children, and schools in the communities that do better? And of particular interest, what are the characteristics that explain why some high-risk communities do unexpectedly well? These questions can only be investigated with population-wide data.

- *Understanding the state of early childhood development in special populations.* Within each country there are special subpopulations, or specific populations defined by geography, language background, or economic circumstances. Child development outcomes tend to vary across such population groups. Quantification of the relative and absolute differences across these groups, as well as the variation in results within special populations, are of interest, and can reveal patterns that lead to a better understanding of the determinants of early education and inform public policies for these groups.

- *Anchoring developmental trajectories to help evaluate early childhood policies, interventions, and programs.* Instruments that measure child development, as opposed to developmental pathology, are able to place individual children on a developmental continuum. As such, it is easier to anchor a child's developmental trajectory as well as make it easier to assess how that child continues to develop over time. Such scales improve our ability to evaluate policies, interventions, and programs.

- *Informing community development and policy.* Policy making, service planning, and community development strategies are increasingly required to be based on evidence. Evidence based on population-level data can help achieve recognition of a policy issue. The extent and nature of the problems can be quantified to inform the policy actions required.

- *Understanding culture.* To better understand and unpack the influence of culture, research studies comparing migrant populations to the population of "home origin" are also becoming more common with the use of internationally comparable population measures. Doing this enables us to better understand how cultural practices affect child development both positively and negatively. And by using the same instrument across countries, we can also start to investigate contexts that are country specific.

- *International comparison.* International comparisons can act as a strong catalyst and advocacy tool. Such data can lead to a better understanding of how macro-level policies affect families and children. For example, maternity/paternity leave entitlements, minimum wage standards, preschool availability, minimum-level teacher qualifications in early education, and education standards, which all tend to be nationwide policies, can be better evaluated when internationally comparable measures are used over time.

CHAPTER 3

Steps in the Development of the Tongan Early Human Capability Index

Why Develop a New Measure of Early Human Capability for Tonga?

The United Nations Secretary General in 2010 stated that "to better monitor children's rights to develop to their full potential, an internationally agreed set of core indicators needs to be established and reported upon regularly" (United Nations 2010). However, despite the acknowledged benefits, no single internationally recognized measure exists. That is not to say there are no measures to assess child developmental delay and disabilities, but that no measure has been developed with the specific intent to measure early human capability (that is, the strengths of children and not just the deficits). Because of the lack of such an instrument, researchers are using instruments that do not meet their needs and are not fit-for-purpose.

The aims of most early childhood interventions, including the Pacific Early Age Readiness and Learning (PEARL) Programme, are to support early human capability and not simply to prevent disability or delay. Thus there was a need for an outcome measure that could capture both developmental delay and strengths. Current child development measures based on milestones and pass/fail outcomes generally lack the sensitivity required for the evaluation of early childhood development (enhancement) interventions and the range to determine the impact of familial and ecological influences on a child. For example, early education and stimulation programs meant to improve the capability of children struggle to find impact using existing developmental milestone-based instruments. An instrument that can measure early human capability, as opposed to developmental pathology, significantly improves our ability to understand the mechanisms behind child development. By measuring both the strengths and weaknesses in children, we can better ask what factors help to support children in some communities in Tonga better than others.

Some researchers and governments use the Early Development Instrument (EDI), which is one of the few measures of child development that is holistic and not solely aimed at capturing developmental delay. The EDI has been used in over 20 countries, with Australia and Canada the biggest adopters (Janus, Brinkman, and Duku 2011). In Australia, the EDI is more commonly known as the Australian Early Development Census, which is implemented as a developmental census across the country once every three years. The EDI has shown reliability and validity in many countries (Andrich and Styles 2004; Brinkman and Blackmore 2003; Brinkman and others 2007, 2013). However, the EDI was developed as a population measure to measure school readiness in the Canadian school system (Janus and Offord 2007), and although it was fairly easily translated into the Australian context (Goldfeld and others 2009), it was never intended as a measure of early human capability for international use across diverse cultures. Tonga required an instrument that was reliable and valid for the local culture and context, but unfortunately aspects of the EDI do not work as well in non-Western cultures. For example, the original intent of the EDI question "coming to school dressed appropriately" was to capture children who are disorganized, rather than children that may come from a poor family who cannot afford "appropriate" clothes. Another example is "stopping a quarrel or dispute," considered a positive attribute in the Western frame of the EDI. But in the Pacific and in some Asian and Latin American cultures, this is seen as a negative attribute; indeed, it is a sign of respect to not get involved in other people's disputes. Considering these limitations, the EDI was not considered appropriate for Tonga.

The aim for Tonga was to not only develop a measure of early human capability that is locally relevant but, uniquely, to build local capacity and systems to use the instrument to monitor early child development over time. The data resulting from the instrument was to support and inform the development of interventions and programs. Additionally, the instrument was to be developed with multiple purposes in mind: (1) population monitoring and surveillance; (2) impact evaluation of the school readiness component of the PEARL program; and (3) as a baseline for a longitudinal cohort study to predict the future capabilities and capacities of children, particularly the later reading and literacy skills that are crucial outcomes to the second component of the PEARL program.

Consultations: What Does a "Solid/Strong" Tongan Child Look Like When Starting School?

Consultation with local stakeholders is key to any successful adaptation or development of a new locally relevant measure of child development (Herdman, Fox-Rushby, and Badia 1997, 1998). The process of validating an instrument requires a series of steps to be taken before a sufficient level of confidence can be placed in the tool and, subsequently, inferences can be made about the children based on the scores or results from the instrument. Invalid measures can either inflate or hide true differences in child development, and what may be a reliable measure of child development in one culture may not work in another. Where pragmatic, the International Test Commission guidelines for the development of psychological and educational tests was adhered to (International Test Commission 2005).

The steps undertaken in Tonga included a series of local consultations to ensure content and face validity, and to ensure the translations were capturing the true essence and intent of each item. The instrument was then piloted for determining the most efficient and reliable method of data collection, and to determine whether the scale distributions were discriminating, as would be expected, and whether they were suffering from ceiling or floor problems for the targeted age range. The implementation of the full developmental census then rendered sufficient data for the instrument to be psychometrically tested with Rasch modeling. These steps are now described in more detail.

Step 1: First Consultations

The concepts that define the dimensions of child development and school readiness are not consistent across cultures, and as such significant consultations with stakeholders were undertaken to understand what were considered to be the "building blocks" for a school-ready child in Tonga. Further local consultation was undertaken throughout the adaptation process to ensure that local cultural aspects and values around child development were being properly captured.

Initial discussions were facilitated with the Ministry of Education and Training, Ministry of Health, church leaders, and other locally identified stakeholders on the concepts of school readiness, and on methods of how to measure school readiness. Discussions centered on "what a solid/strong child in Tonga would look like at school entry." It was agreed after these initial discussions that the following domains of development were to be captured by the instrument:

- Communication skills
- Language and cognitive skills
- Approaches to learning
- Cultural identity and spirituality
- Social and emotional skills
- Physical health

It was also important to understand the local early education settings, coverage, and program/system aims before developing the content of the instrument, and also the best method for administering a population-wide data collection. In Tonga, some children enter early learning programs at ages three to four, but the coverage is not consistent across the island groups. Many areas have no early learning program or services, and of those that do exist, the quality varies dramatically. The Ministry of Education and Training was aware of the range of services available and the inconsistent coverage of service provision. The Parliament of Tonga was also in the process of changing legislation to reduce the mandatory age of formal schooling to four years of age, which meant that early childhood education was to fall under the mandate of the ministry. Considering all these factors, it was clear to all stakeholders that the development and first use of the Tongan Early Human Capability Index (TeHCI) would occur before major changes in the early education system. Most stakeholders were excited that the TeHCI would not only evaluate PEARL but also other early education policy changes. Stakeholders felt that the instrument should also be used to show the areas of child development that may require greatest support in Tonga, and thus the resultant data could also be used to support the development of curriculum and program planning for the new services.

Once both the aims of the instrument and the breadth of development to be captured were clear, the consultation process moved onto identifying the specific items under each of the broader domains to cover. Essentially a "shopping list" of approximately 130 items was generated through this initial consultation process. The list was then matched as best as possible to other international measures to develop a draft instrument.

This was developed on the basis of the feedback from the local consultations in Tonga and was cognizant of the child development measurement literature. The draft instrument also aimed to reduce social desirability response bias, and was attuned to modern survey instrument design. It also included questions on service participation and the home environment.

The draft instrument was independently reviewed by two highly respected colleagues (a community paediatrician and an early childhood consultant), who provided unofficial feedback to determine its appropriateness for children ages three to five. They agreed that the items within each of the domains spanned the developmental expectations of children though this age range. Along with the instrument itself, a manual was developed to go alongside the instrument to help facilitate understanding of the intent of the questions. This first draft of the TeHCI was then translated into Tongan.

Step 2: Second Consultation/Face Validity

It was important that the local stakeholders, who were originally consulted before the instrument's development, be consulted again. The aim was for them to review the instrument and ensure that the essence and main aspects of child development that were important for Tongans were still being captured. The aim by the end of this second consultation was also to determine who would administer the TeHCI, and whether the methodology of data collection would need to differ in different localities considering the existing levels of early child care and education services across the country.

A one-day workshop was conducted with the stakeholders who were originally consulted to present the first draft of the TeHCI, along with its translation into Tongan for further feedback and reflection on the instrument. On the basis of feedback from the workshop, a second version of the TeHCI was developed in

Tongan, and then translated again into English and Tongan to check that the intent of the questions was still being captured. At this stage, the badging of the instrument as the TeHCI was secured, and the Tongan country logo was added to the first page of the instrument.

Step 3: Pilot Test

The TeHCI was then piloted to determine the instrument's "ceiling" and "floor" on each of the scales for children ages three to five (that is, the scales were not too hard or soft, and captured the full developmental range of children in Tonga). The pilot also aimed to determine if the translation was working well, and if parents and teachers found the questions easy to answer.

In total 250 questionnaires were completed through the pilot, conducted on the islands of Tongatapu, Vava'u, and 'Atata. The data collection included a mix of administration methods including:

- Teacher completed
- Caregiver completed
- Interview with caregiver (survey style)
- Facilitated caregiver completed (mothers/caregivers complete the instrument question by question as described by the facilitator)

Within the islands and communities, meetings were held with local child health nurses, teachers, school staff, town officers, and town governor officers to determine the best method and process for implementing the TeHCI at community level.

To support the ongoing local capacity building around the development of not only the TeHCI itself but also the establishment of a full monitoring system, a database for data collection was developed locally with technical support from the lead author. Data entry was completed by local early education students from the Teacher Institute of Education, as well as some high school students. Data analyses were conducted in the statistical software package since this is the main statistical package used by the University of the South Pacific and, as such, the statistical package for which there is local knowledge and capacity.

The pilot results showed that some of the scales were working well, while others were "too easy," showing a ceiling on the scales, particularly for the verbal scale. The results also showed that some of the scales discriminated better than others by the age and gender of the child and education of the mother. In all circumstances, however, the directions of the discrimination were in the expected direction, giving confidence in the properties of the instrument.

The pilot process also revealed that the most efficient and reliable method of data collection and implementation of the TeHCI was a mixed-method approach. A data collection protocol was developed whereby teachers would complete the TeHCI for children attending some form of early education program. In all other cases, the TeHCI would be implemented at community level. This was to be facilitated by calling a village or town meeting with mothers, the latter being called by the town officer. The TeHCI would then be completed by mothers at the community meeting, and those who did not attend the meeting were followed up at home to complete the TeHCI. The community implementation would be undertaken in partnership between health and education sectors through local child health nurses and teachers.

Step 4: Third Consultation to Finalize Instrument

A one-day workshop was facilitated presenting the results of the pilot back to the original group of stakeholders, as well as others who had developed an interest in the activities. Some stakeholders involved in the original consultations brought with them other staff and stakeholders showing interest, which provided an opportunity for further capacity development. After further discussion by the group additional items were developed and a few original items dropped. The translated instrument was carefully reviewed again, especially for questions that were a bit harder for the parents and caregivers to understand. This then created the third and final version of the TeHCI (see appendix A). The TeHCI manual was also edited to reflect the changes.

The TeHCI

The resultant instrument after consultation and piloting captured the following domains of development:

- Physical health
- Verbal communication
- Cultural identity and spirituality
- Social and emotional well-being and skills
- Perseverance and approaches to learning
- Numeracy and concepts
- Literacy (reading and writing)

In addition to the questions on child development, the instrument captured basic background characteristics on the child, the primary caregiver's educational level, and some questions on early childhood education attendance and the home environment. The full list is shown in table 3.1.

For those familiar with measures of child development, a number of items will be recognizably similar to existing instrumentation. In particular, those in the EDI and the Ages and Stages Questionnaires allowed for some international benchmarking. However, the intention of the TeHCI was that it be culturally and contextually relevant for Tonga, over and above international comparison.

Table 3.1 Tongan Early Human Capability Index Questionnaire Items

Background information

Child's name

Child's date of birth

Child's gender

Education level of child's primary caregiver

Community where child lives

Physical health

Child's height

Child's weight

Does this child have any disabilities/special needs (or needs help with)?

What disabilities?

Is this child sickly or looked after poorly?

Does this child have good hygiene; that is, always washes his/her hands after toileting?

Does this child have positive habits "mafai"/"fili fakapotopoto"?

Does this child know good foods from bad foods?

General verbal communication

Can this child use a group of words in talking?

Can this child converse with others?

Can this child talk about something that he/she has done?

Can this child give detail with good Tongan words?

Can this child hold an adult-like conversation (for example, talkative, always questioning)?

Cultural identity and spirituality

Does this child show compassion, understanding, and tolerance of others?

Can this child identify two culturally important foods/fruits?

Can this child identify two local plants that provide foods/fruits?

Does this child show the Tongan cultural values of humility?

Does this child show the Tongan cultural values of devotion/commitment/obligation/responsibility?

Does this child show the Tongan cultural values of reciprocity in relationships?

Does this child participate in cultural routines?

Is this child able to say a short prayer?

Social and emotional well-being and skills

Is the child happy to share his/her toys and belongings?

Does this child take care of his/her own things?

Does this child demonstrate respect for adults?

Does this child demonstrate respect for other children?

Does this child accept responsibility for his/her actions?

Is this child considerate of other people's feelings?

Does this child repeatedly do something wrong even though he/she has been told to stop?

Is this child always helpful?

Is this child friendly to other children?

Does this child kick, bite, or hit adults or other children?

Is this child impatient?

Does this child always understand the difference between right and wrong?

Does this child follow simple directions on how to do something?

table continues next page

Table 3.1 Tongan Early Human Capability Index Questionnaire Items *(continued)*

Perseverance

Does this child always perform tasks independently?

Does this child always keep at a task until it is finished?

Does this child need constant reminding to finish something off?

Does this child get easily distracted from a task?

Approaches to learning

Does this child show more curiosity about something new in comparison to something familiar?

Does this child investigate/explore the function of a new toy/game/puzzle or object?

Is this child always wanting to learn new things?

When in an unfamiliar environment with a familiar person present, does this child feel free to explore?

Is this child always diligent in his/her approach to a new job or task?

Numeracy and concepts

Can this child recognize geometric shapes (for example, triangle, circle, square)?

Can this child name and identify at least three colors?

Can this child sort and classify objects by common characteristics (for example, shape, color, size)?

Can this child name and recognize the symbol of all numbers from 1 to 10?

Can this child count to 10?

Can this child count to 20?

Can this child count to 100?

Does this child know that a horse is taller than a dog?

Does this child know the order of the day (for example, morning, then afternoon, and then evening)?

Does this child understand the concepts of yesterday, today, and tomorrow?

Does this child know that a vehicle weighs more than a cup?

Does the child know that the number 8 is bigger than the number 2?

Formal literacy: reading

Does this child know the sounds of three letters of the alphabet (phonics)?

Can this child identify at least 3 letters of the alphabet?

Can this child identify at least 10 letters of the alphabet?

Are there any reading materials in the child's home (for example, picture books, magazines)?

Can this child hold a book and turn the pages in the right way?

Can this child follow reading directions (that is, left to right, top to bottom)?

Can this child read at least four simple popular words?

Formal literacy: writing

Can this child draw something identifiable (for example, a stick person)?

Can this child copy (trace) the shape of a letter (for example, A, E, F)?

Can this child write his/her own name?

Can this child write short and simple words?

Can this child write short and simple sentences?

General questions: early childhood education participation

Does/did this child attend kindergarten/playgroup?

If yes, what year did he/she start?

If yes, how long did he/she go for?

If yes, give the name of the kindergarten/playgroup and why you sent them there

If no, why didn't this child go to kindergarten/playgroup?

table continues next page

Table 3.1 Tongan Early Human Capability Index Questionnaire Items *(continued)*

General questions: home environment

In the past three days did you or any household member over the age of 15 engage in the following activities with your child?

Read books or looked at picture books with

Told stories to

Sang songs to/or with

Played with

Named, counted, or drew things to/with

Implementation of the Census

The TeHCI census ended up being completed in two separate stages because of Cyclone Ian causing widespread destruction in Tonga in January 2014. The data collection for the 'Eua and Ha'apai island groups was begun in the two months before Cyclone Ian, but had to be put on hold as all government staff, especially those in cyclone-hit communities, prioritized rebuilding and reconstruction efforts. Data collection resumed in March 2014 and was completed in May 2014. Data were captured from all 36 inhabited islands. Using figures from the 2011 Tongan Population Census (currently the most comprehensive data to estimate a population denominator from), it is estimated that the survey captured approximately 81 percent of all children ages three to five across Tonga.

Early Childhood Development in Tonga • http://dx.doi.org/10.1596/978-1-4648-0999-6

CHAPTER 4

Results

Resultant Sample Description

The baseline Tongan Early Human Capability Index (TeHCI) data collection achieved a sample of 6,604 children. Enumeration data are not available in Tonga, and data collected through birth registrations or community health nurses were not electronically recorded. The TeHCI was collected in late 2013 and early 2014. On the basis of the number of children ages one to three in the 2011 census we expected there would be 8,136 children ages three to five during the period of data collection, assuming a stagnant population (that is, no net migration in or out of the country and no deaths). When broken down to the main island groups, the estimated participation rate ranged from 79.7 percent to 84.8 percent (table 4.1).

The sample characteristics were representative of the 2011 census. As already noted, the sample aimed to collect data for children ages three to five; however, 189 children ages six were swept up in the data collection. These children were primarily attending some form of preschool and were collected through the teacher-completed checklists. Although 95 percent of these children had only recently turned six (within the previous two months), they were excluded from any further analyses shown in the sample characteristics in table 4.2.

TeHCI Descriptive Results

For each of the TeHCI domains, the scores range from 0 through to 1, with 1 being the best score and 0 the worst. The data are not weighted or age standard-ized. As such, as children get older they should show progression up the scales on each of the TeHCI domains. Table 4.3 shows the highest and lowest score (scale range) for each of the domains, the 25th and 75th percentile (interquartile range), the mean/average score, and the standard deviation around the mean. The results are for the whole sample; that is, all children ages three to five across Tonga who participated in the developmental census.

The results presented in table 4.3 indicate that the verbal scale is highly skewed to the right, indicating that most children are performing very well on this scale.

Table 4.1 Estimated Participation Rate by Main Island Group

Island group	Sample	Expected number	Estimated participation rate (%)
Tongatapu	4,806	5,962	80.6
Vava'u	1,005	1,185	84.8
'Eua	3,060	384	79.7
Ha'apai	418	521	80.2
Niuas	69	84	82.1
Tonga overall	6,604	8,136	81.1

Table 4.2 Sample Characteristics

Characteristic	Number (%)
Gender	
Male	3,443 (52.1)
Female	3,161 (47.9)
Age	
3 years	1,790 (27.1)
4 years	2,186 (33.1)
5 years	2,380 (36.0)
6 years	189 (2.9)
Missing	59 (0.1)
Special needs	
Identified by respondent	534 (8.1)
Not identified	6,042 (91.5)
Missing	28 (0.4)
Mothers education level	
Primary	84 (1.3)
Started high school	2,534 (38.4)
Completed high school	2,794 (42.3)
Postschool education	1,186 (18.0)
Missing	6 (0.1)

Table 4.3 Tongan Early Human Capability Index Descriptive Results

Domain	Min	25th percentile	Mean	SD	75th percentile	Max	Missing	Number valid
Physical	0	0.50	0.73	0.27	1.00	1	39	6,317
Verbal	0	0.80	0.85	0.23	1.00	1	24	6,332
Cultural and spirituality	0	0.50	0.68	0.27	1.00	1	52	6,304
Social and emotional	0	0.54	0.68	0.21	0.85	1	49	6,307
Perseverance	0	0.25	0.45	0.25	0.50	1	21	6,335
Approaches	0	0.60	0.72	0.33	1.00	1	28	6,328
Numbers and concepts	0	0.25	0.48	0.30	0.75	1	59	6,297
Literacy	0	0.17	0.44	0.31	0.68	1	51	6,305

Note: SD = standard deviation.

Early Childhood Development in Tonga • http://dx.doi.org/10.1596/978-1-4648-0999-6

This is indicative of the developmental domain and the age of the children, with most children above age three showing good verbal communication skills. The physical health domain score is also skewed to the right, indicating that most children are doing well on this scale. These results are as expected considering the age range of the children and the items assessed within the domains. Despite the skew, there is still room for improvement on the verbal and the physical scales of development. For the other domains, there was a concerted effort during the TeHCI's development and piloting to capture the wide range of development that children can show during this age range. The results shown in table 4.3 show wider interquartile range for these domains. These results and those shown in the rest of the tables in this chapter indicate the TeHCI is capturing a wide range of development, and that the instrument is sensitive enough to enable discrimination by age, gender, and mother's educational level. The results of the Rasch modeling in appendix C provide further confidence in the scaling properties of the TeHCI, and that the instrument will be sensitive to change.

Social and Demographic Factors Affect Child Development

As expected, we find that in Tonga development improves as children age (table 4.4). Indeed, progression up the scales of the TeHCI can be seen for all domains of development as children get older. These improvements by age are highly statistically significant and show linearity in the direction expected (that is, the older the child, the better they do). Analyses of variance statistics were applied to compare the mean results.

Also as expected, and consistent with the child development literature, girls outperform boys across all domains of development, except for approaches to learning where there is no real difference. Analyses of variance statistics were applied to compare the mean results; the F values and significance are provided (table 4.5).

Table 4.4 Child Development by Age

Age		Physical	Verbal	Cultural/ spiritual	Social/ emotional	Perseverance	Approaches	Numeracy/ concepts	Literacy
3	Mean (SD)	0.64	0.79	0.58	0.61	0.39	0.63	0.27	0.23
		(0.27)	(0.26)	(0.28)	(0.21)	(0.25)	(0.35)	(0.23)	(0.21)
	N	1,775	1,783	1,774	1,776	1,782	1,780	1,767	1,772
4	Mean (SD)	0.72	0.84	0.67	0.67	0.45	0.71	0.44	0.37
		(0.27)	(0.22)	(0.27)	(0.21)	(0.25)	(0.33)	(0.27)	(0.27)
	N	2,175	2,176	2,171	2,169	2,180	2,180	2,169	2,170
5	Mean (SD)	0.80	0.89	0.75	0.73	0.49	0.78	0.68	0.65
		(0.24)	(0.19)	(0.24)	(0.19)	(0.24)	(0.29)	(0.25)	(0.29)
	N	2,367	2,373	2,359	2,362	2,373	2,368	2,361	2,363
ANOVA	F	376.5	225.7	410.1	309.3	145.8	239.2	2,824.9	2,753.6
	Sig	0.000	0.000	0.000	0.000	0.000	0.000	0.000	0.000

Note: ANOVA = analysis of variance; F = F statistic; N = number of children; SD = standard deviation.

Table 4.5 Child Development by Gender

Sex		Physical	Verbal	Cultural/ spiritual	Social/ emotional	Perseverance	Approaches	Numeracy/ concepts	Literacy
Boy	Mean (SD)	0.71	0.84	0.67	0.66	0.44	0.71	0.47	0.41
		(0.27)	(0.23)	(0.28)	(0.21)	(0.25)	(0.33)	(0.30)	(0.31)
	N	3,318	3,325	3,306	3,306	3,326	3,319	3,309	3,307
Girl	Mean (SD)	0.75	0.86	0.69	0.69	0.47	0.72	0.51	0.46
		(0.26)	(0.22)	(0.27)	(0.21)	(0.25)	(0.33)	(0.30)	(0.32)
	N	2,999	3,007	2,998	3,001	3,009	3,009	2,988	2,998
ANOVA	F	39.9	14.4	12.9	30.1	19.9	0.6	26.5	33.6
	Sig	0.000	0.000	0.000	0.000	0.000	0.440	0.000	0.000

Note: ANOVA = analysis of variance; F = F statistic; N = number of children; SD = standard deviation.

In Tonga, children are more likely to do better on all aspects of child development if their primary caregiver has a higher educational background. Note that from this point forward in the report, the primary caregiver is referred to as the "mother" of the child, recognizing that this may not always be the biological mother of the child. It is not uncommon in Tonga for children to be raised by aunts or other family members. The relationship between child development and mother's education is so marked that for every jump in mother's educational level there is an incremental jump in child development, showing a statistically significant linear relationship for every domain. Again, these results are very consistent with international findings. One of many drivers behind international efforts to improve educational outcomes for women is this relationship with child development. Mothers with higher educational levels will generally be able to generate greater levels of resources to support their families, and they also have more taught skills to be able to pass on through everyday stimulation and interaction with their children. As shown in table 4.6, the relationship between mother's education and child development in Tonga is more pronounced for the domains of physical health, approaches to learning, numeracy and concepts, and literacy skills. Analyses of variance statistics were applied to compare the mean results; the F values and significance are provided.

Table 4.7 shows a relatively inconsistent variation in child development across Tonga's main island groups. Children residing in the main island of Tongatapu show better development for physical health, but—perhaps unexpectedly—not higher levels of development across the other domains. Before the data were collected, it was expected that children in Tongatapu would do better relative to the other island groups because they may have greater access to resources and services than the outer islands. However, children in the Niuas, the most remote of the island groups, showed the strongest results for verbal skills, literacy, numeracy and concepts, approaches to learning, and perseverance. These results indicate that programs with universal coverage (that is, to support all island groups across Tonga) are warranted, with little evidence to support programs that only target specific island groups. It should also be noted that when analyzed in a single model together, mother's education is the strongest predictor of a child's

Table 4.6 Child Development by Educational Attainment of Child's Mother

Mother's education		Physical	Verbal	Cultural/ spiritual	Social/ emotional	Perseverance	Approaches	Numeracy/ concepts	Literacy
Primary	Mean (SD)	0.59 (0.30)	0.80 (0.29)	0.61 (0.30)	0.61 (0.24)	0.42 (0.25)	0.61 (0.38)	0.40 (0.34)	0.34 (0.32)
	N	79	79	80	79	80	80	80	79
Started high school	Mean (SD)	0.69 (0.28)	0.83 (0.23)	0.64 (0.28)	0.64 (0.22)	0.43 (0.25)	0.67 (0.34)	0.43 (0.30)	0.38 (0.30)
	N	2,433	2,436	2,434	2,429	2,439	2,436	2,424	2,429
Completed high school	Mean (SD)	0.74 (0.26)	0.86 (0.22)	0.69 (0.26)	0.69 (0.20)	0.46 (0.24)	0.73 (0.32)	0.51 (0.30)	0.46 (0.31)
	N	2,678	2,688	2,666	2,678	2,688	2,681	2,670	2,674
Tertiary	Mean (SD)	0.79 (0.25)	0.87 (0.22)	0.73 (0.27)	0.72 (0.72)	0.47 (0.26)	0.78 (0.29)	0.55 (0.30)	0.50 (0.31)
ANOVA	N	1,121	1,123	1,118	1,115	1,122	1,125	1,117	1,117
	F	126.4	29.6	113.2	126.1	30.6	97.7	144.5	130.9
	Sig	0.000	0.000	0.000	0.000	0.000	0.000	0.000	0.000

Note: ANOVA = analysis of variance; F = F statistic; N = number of children; SD = standard deviation.

Table 4.7 Child Development by Island Group of Residence

Island group		Physical	Verbal	Cultural/ spiritual	Social/ emotional	Perseverance	Approaches	Numeracy/ concepts	Literacy
Tongatapu	Mean (SD)	0.74 (0.26)	0.84 (0.23)	0.69 (0.28)	0.68 (0.21)	0.44 (0.25)	0.73 (0.33)	0.49 (0.30)	0.44 (0.31)
	N	4,610	4,610	4,598	4,597	4,611	4,606	4,592	4,589
Vava'u	Mean (SD)	0.70 (0.28)	0.89 (0.19)	0.63 (0.24)	0.69 (0.20)	0.49 (0.24)	0.67 (0.32)	0.46 (0.30)	0.43 (0.31)
	N	953	951	950	948	953	952	951	952
'Eua	Mean (SD)	0.71 (0.27)	0.84 (0.22)	0.68 (0.27)	0.68 (0.20)	0.46 (0.24)	0.73 (0.30)	0.54 (0.29)	0.44 (0.30)
	N	290	296	286	291	294	296	288	289
Ha'apai	Mean (SD)	0.65 (0.27)	0.82 (0.22)	0.61 (0.28)	0.62 (0.21)	0.46 (0.25)	0.68 (0.33)	0.45 (0.29)	0.40 (0.32)
	N	400	406	403	403	409	406	403	406
Niuatoputapu	Mean (SD)	0.59 (0.18)	0.87 (0.18)	0.69 (0.19)	0.58 (0.20)	0.48 (0.34)	0.81 (0.20)	0.60 (0.26)	0.49 (0.25)
	N	46	51	49	50	50	50	45	51
Niuafo'ou	Mean (SD)	0.69 (0.30)	0.91 (0.12)	0.68 (0.29)	0.68 (0.16)	0.54 (0.23)	0.86 (0.20)	0.63 (0.29)	0.64 (0.28)
	N	18	18	18	18	18	18	18	18
ANOVA	F	15.7	8.8	14.4	7.7	6.9	6.9	6.4	3.0
	Sig	0.000	0.000	0.000	0.000	0.000	0.000	0.000	0.000

Note: ANOVA = analysis of variance; F = F statistic; N = number of children; SD = standard deviation.

development even though the island of residence still accounts for some degree of statistical significance. In table 4.7, analyses of variance statistics were applied to compare the mean results; the F values and significance are provided.

Early Childhood Stimulation in the Home Positively Affects Child Development

The TeHCI includes a standard set of questions used by UNICEF's Multiple Indicator Cluster Survey. These ask the primary caregivers if they or any family member aged over 15 have undertaken various activities with the child during the last week. The questions are meant to provide a general indicator of the level of stimulation and interaction that families have with their children to support everyday learning in the home environment. Figure 4.1 represents the percentage of children ages three to five for whom these activities were provided.

A closer look at these results find the likelihood of children having higher levels of interaction and stimulation in the home is related to the mother's educational level. Indeed, the relationship between the mother's educational level and interactions in the home environment with the child is linear, as can be seen in figure 4.2. The linear relationship is most pronounced for reading with the child, where only 42 percent of children born to a mother with primary school education were involved in reading activities in the home compared to 72 percent of children born to mothers with tertiary-level qualifications. These results likely reflect the literacy levels of caregivers influencing their likelihood to read to their own children.

Figure 4.1 Activities in the Home Environment for Children Ages 3–5

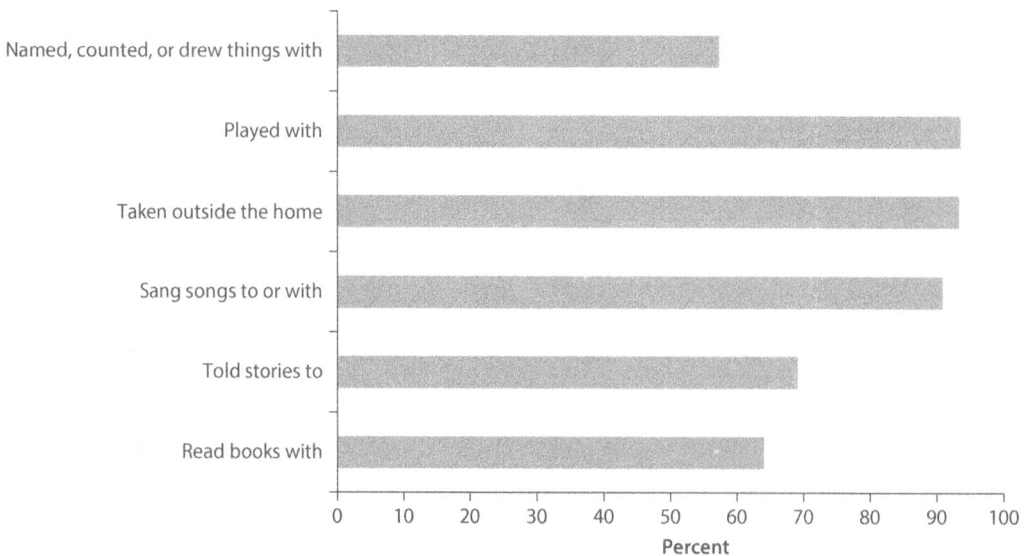

Figure 4.2 Activities in the Child's Home Environment by Mother's Education Level

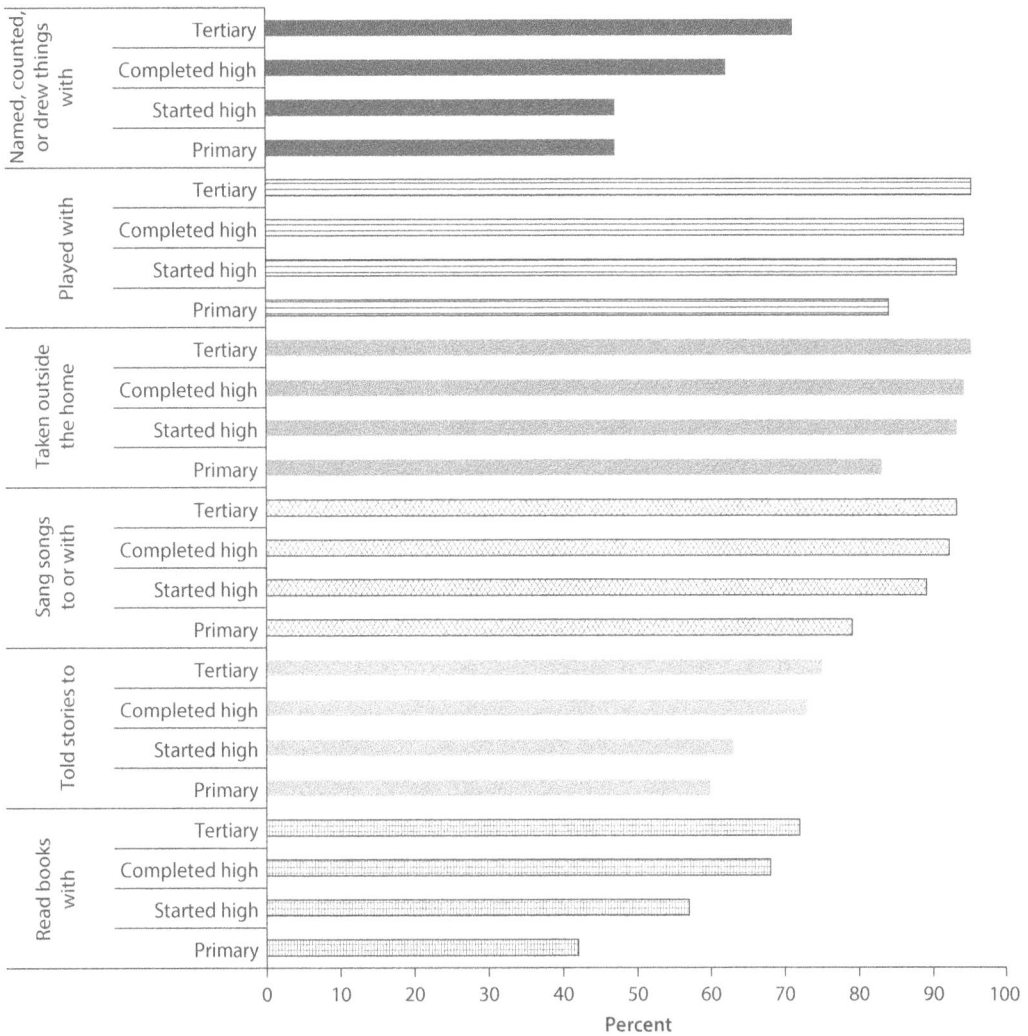

Tables 4.8–4.15 explore the relationship between these activities in the home environment and a child's development. As expected, children have higher literacy levels if they come from households where they have been read to; however, higher levels of development can be seen for these children across all the developmental domains. This likely reflects a more interactive and supportive home environment for healthy development. Indeed, tables 4.8–4.15 all show the same trend; that is, children who are interacted with in the home environment show better levels of development for every aspect of development. Analyses of variance models were applied to compare the mean results, while controlling for mothers' educational level; the F values and significance are provided in all these tables. The consistency across these tables is a strong

Table 4.8 Relationship between Reading in the Home Environment and Child Development

Read books or looked at picture books		Physical	Verbal	Cultural/ spiritual	Social/ emotional	Perseverance	Approaches	Numeracy/ concepts	Literacy
Yes	Mean (SD)	0.77 (0.25)	0.89 (0.19)	0.73 (0.25)	0.71 (0.19)	0.47 (0.24)	0.77 (0.29)	0.54 (0.29)	0.50 (0.31)
	N	3,609	3,615	3,600	3,604	3,615	3,613	3,600	3,603
No	Mean (SD)	0.63 (0.28)	0.79 (0.26)	0.58 (0.29)	0.60 (0.21)	0.40 (0.24)	0.60 (0.35)	0.33 (0.26)	0.27 (0.26)
	N	2,025	2,028	2,024	2,022	2,031	2,030	2,028	2,027
ANOVA	F	194.7	133.9	210.5	193.3	52.8	175.2	374.7	411.3
	Sig	0.000	0.000	0.000	0.000	0.000	0.000	0.000	0.000

Note: ANOVA = analysis of variance; F = F statistic; N = number of children; SD = standard deviation.

Table 4.9 Relationship between Reading in the Home Environment and Child Development for Children Not Attending Preschool

Read books or looked at picture books		Physical	Verbal	Cultural/ spiritual	Social/ emotional	Perseverance	Approaches	Numeracy/ concepts	Literacy
Yes	Mean (SD)	0.75 (0.26)	0.88 (0.19)	0.71 (0.25)	0.69 (0.19)	0.47 (0.23)	0.74 (0.31)	0.49 (0.30)	0.45 (0.31)
	N	2,114	2,118	2,104	2,109	2,118	2,114	2,108	2,113
No	Mean (SD)	0.60 (0.27)	0.78 (0.26)	0.57 (0.29)	0.59 (0.27)	0.40 (0.23)	0.59 (0.36)	0.29 (0.25)	0.24 (0.25)
	N	1,508	1,513	1,511	1,508	1,513	1,513	1,512	1,509
ANOVA	F	113.8	77.6	111.9	117.7	34.1	97.2	206.3	230.4
	Sig	0.000	0.000	0.000	0.000	0.000	0.000	0.000	0.000

Note: ANOVA = analysis of variance; F = F statistic; N = number of children; SD = standard deviation.

Table 4.10 Relationship between Reading in the Home Environment and Child Development for Children Attending Preschool

Read books or looked at picture books		Physical	Verbal	Cultural/ spiritual	Social/ emotional	Perseverance	Approaches	Numeracy/ concepts	Literacy
Yes	Mean (SD)	0.81 (0.23)	0.90 (0.17)	0.76 (0.22)	0.73 (0.62)	0.47 (0.25)	0.80 (0.27)	0.63 (0.26)	0.60 (0.29)
	N	1,687	1,690	1,687	1,686	1,690	1,691	1,685	1,683
No	Mean (SD)	0.69 (0.27)	0.81 (0.24)	0.61 (0.29)	0.62 (00.21)	0.39 (0.24)	0.64 (0.33)	0.42 (0.26)	0.36 (0.28)
	N	561	559	557	558	562	561	560	561
ANOVA	F	113.8	77.6	111.9	117.7	34.1	97.2	206.3	230.4
	Sig	0.000	0.000	0.000	0.000	0.000	0.000	0.000	0.000

Note: ANOVA = analysis of variance; F = F statistic; N = number of children; SD = standard deviation.

Table 4.11 Relationship between Telling Stories in the Home Environment and Child Development

Told stories to		Physical	Verbal	Cultural/ spiritual	Social/ emotional	Perseverance	Approaches	Numeracy/ concepts	Literacy
Yes	Mean (SD)	0.76 (0.26)	0.88 (0.19)	0.72 (0.25)	0.70 (0.19)	0.47 (0.24)	0.76 (0.30)	0.52 (0.29)	0.48 (0.31)
	N	3,900	3,902	3,891	3,892	3,902	3,905	3,895	3,893
No	Mean (SD)	0.63 (0.28)	0.78 (0.27)	0.57 (0.29)	0.60 (0.22)	0.41 (0.25)	0.58 (0.36)	0.33 (0.27)	0.28 (0.26)
	N	1,737	1,743	1,735	1,736	1,746	1,740	1,735	1,739
ANOVA	F	295.6	260.1	412.4	273.3	72.7	384.0	535.9	544.9
	Sig	0.000	0.000	0.000	0.000	0.000	0.000	0.000	0.000

Note: ANOVA = analysis of variance; F = F statistic; N = number of children; SD = standard deviation.

Table 4.12 Relationship between Singing Songs in the Home Environment and Child Development

Sang song to or with		Physical	Verbal	Cultural/ spiritual	Social/ emotional	Perseverance	Approaches	Numeracy/ concepts	Literacy
Yes	Mean (SD)	0.74 (0.26)	0.87 (0.20)	0.70 (0.26)	0.68 (0.20)	0.45 (0.24)	0.73 (0.32)	0.48 (0.29)	0.44 (0.31)
	N	5,119	5,126	5,122	5,110	5,128	5,125	5,113	5,115
No	Mean (SD)	0.57 (0.28)	0.69 (0.31)	0.46 (0.30)	0.55 (0.23)	0.41 (0.25)	0.50 (0.37)	0.28 (0.28)	0.23 (0.27)
	N	518	521	516	520	522	522	519	519
ANOVA	F	96.2	157.9	183.6	91.5	9.1	120.5	117.2	114.6
	Sig	0.000	0.000	0.000	0.000	0.000	0.000	0.000	0.000

Note: ANOVA = analysis of variance; F = F statistic; N = number of children; SD = standard deviation.

Table 4.13 Relationship between Being Taken Outside the Home/Yard Environment and Child Development

Taken outside the home/yard		Physical	Verbal	Cultural/ spiritual	Social/ emotional	Perseverance	Approaches	Numeracy/ concepts	Literacy
Yes	Mean (SD)	0.73 (0.27)	0.86 (0.21)	0.69 (0.26)	0.68 (0.20)	0.45 (0.24)	0.73 (0.32)	0.48 (0.30)	0.43 (0.31)
	N	5,260	5,269	5,255	5,256	5,272	5,270	5,258	5,261
No	Mean (SD)	0.58 (0.28)	0.69 (0.33)	0.47 (0.31)	0.55 (0.24)	0.44 (0.24)	0.46 (0.37)	0.29 (0.28)	0.23 (0.27)
	N	377	378	383	374	378	377	374	373
ANOVA	F	58.6	120.2	113.9	71.1	1.9	124.9	68.7	76.2
	Sig	0.000	0.000	0.000	0.000	0.152	0.000	0.000	0.000

Note: ANOVA = analysis of variance; F = F statistic; N = number of children; SD = standard deviation.

Table 4.14 Relationship between Playing in the Home Environment and Child Development

Played with		Physical	Verbal	Cultural/ Spiritual	Social/ Emotional	Perseverance	Approaches	Numeracy/ Concepts	Literacy
Yes	Mean (SD)	0.73	0.86	0.69	0.68	0.45	0.72	0.48	0.43
		(0.27)	(0.21)	(0.26)	(0.20)	(0.24)	(0.32)	(0.30)	(0.31)
	N	5,272	5,281	5,266	5,265	5,284	5,282	5,270	5,272
No	Mean (SD)	0.56	0.71	0.49	0.54	0.43	0.48	0.29	0.23
		(0.27)	(0.33)	(0.31)	(0.23)	(0.24)	(0.37)	(0.29)	(0.27)
	N	366	367	363	366	367	366	363	363
ANOVA	F	149.8	175.6	193.9	147.4	2.6	194.5	141.5	150.7
	Sig	0.000	0.000	0.000	0.000	0.104	0.000	0.000	0.000

Note: ANOVA = analysis of variance; F = F statistic; N = number of children; SD = standard deviation.

Table 4.15 Relationship between Naming/Counting or Drawing Things with the Child in the Home Environment and Child Development

Named, counted or drew things to/with		Physical	Verbal	Cultural/ spiritual	Social/ emotional	Perseverance	Approaches	Numeracy/ concepts	Literacy
Yes	Mean (SD)	0.79	0.92	0.76	0.73	0.48	0.79	0.58	0.54
		(0.24)	(0.16)	(0.23)	(0.17)	(0.23)	(0.28)	(0.28)	(0.30)
	N	3,228	3,231	3,225	3,223	3,234	3,235	3,228	3,224
No	Mean (SD)	0.62	0.77	0.56	0.59	0.41	0.60	0.31	0.25
		(0.28)	(0.26)	(0.28)	(0.22)	(0.25)	(0.35)	(0.25)	(0.24)
	N	2,408	2,415	2,402	2,406	2,415	2,411	2,403	2,409
ANOVA	F	295.1	338.2	436.0	357.3	60.5	268.9	710.8	750.1
	Sig	0.000	0.000	0.000	0.000	0.000	0.000	0.000	0.000

Note: ANOVA = analysis of variance; F = F statistic; N = number of children; SD = standard deviation.

indication that improvements in child development will be seen if the Pacific Early Age Readiness and Learning (PEARL) Programme is able to enhance the skills and capacity of caregivers to interact with and stimulate children through such activities in the home environment. Of particular interest to the PEARL program are tables 4.9 and 4.10, showing that the impact of reading in the home environment is actually larger than that of attending preschool (that is, children who attend preschool but are not read to in the home environment show poorer outcomes than those who are read to in the home environment). For children who are not being read to at home, however, the impact of pre-school is positive. These results provide solid evidence for the merit of the PEARL program, particularly the merit behind the community-based play-group model. The results also provide confidence in the TeHCI as an instrument that is sensitive to change.

Preschool Services Positively Affect Child Development

Approximately 44 percent of children in Tonga ages three to five attend some form of preschool, kindergarten, early education center, or playgroup, though this figure varies by age and gender. As figure 4.3 shows, attendance at some form of educational service before school increases as children get closer to school age, and participation rates are higher for girls, especially younger girls. It is important to note, however, these figures indicate that over half of all children in Tonga attend school for the first time with no exposure to any early education program. International literature suggests these children will find it harder to transition into the school environment, and are at a higher risk of early school drop-out and school failure.

Participation in preschool is also influenced by island group. These results indicate that participation in some form of early education program is likely to reflect service availability in addition to the interest or intent of parents to send their children to early education services. One of the most remote islands, Niuatoputapu, shows the highest rates of participation in preschool, whereas Ha'apai, which is fairly remote, shows the lowest rates. This reflects local leadership, as most preschool services across Tonga are community-based, thus requiring local leadership and support. Figure 4.4 shows that the age trend—those closer to school age are more likely to attend educational services prior to school—is consistent across each of the island groups except for Niuafo'ou. However, Niuafo'ou has only 18 children, being by far the least populated region disaggregated in the TeHCI results.

Figure 4.3 **Preschool Participation by Age and Sex**

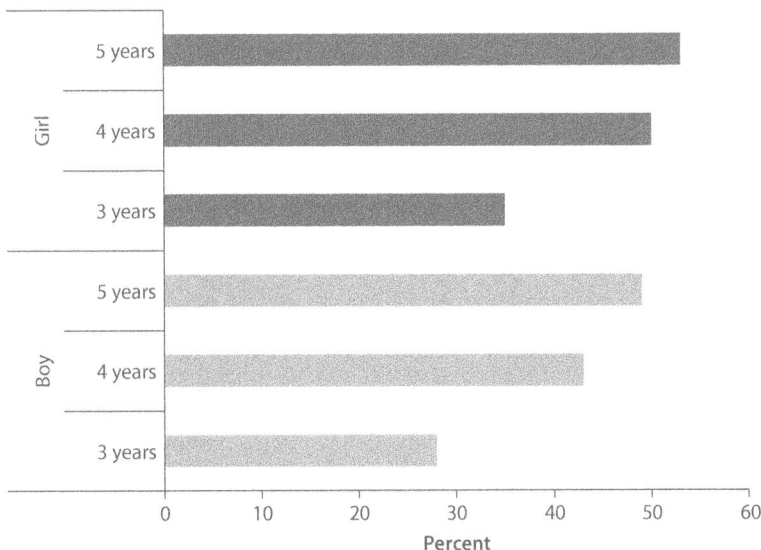

Early Childhood Development in Tonga • http://dx.doi.org/10.1596/978-1-4648-0999-6

Figure 4.4 Preschool Participation by Island Group

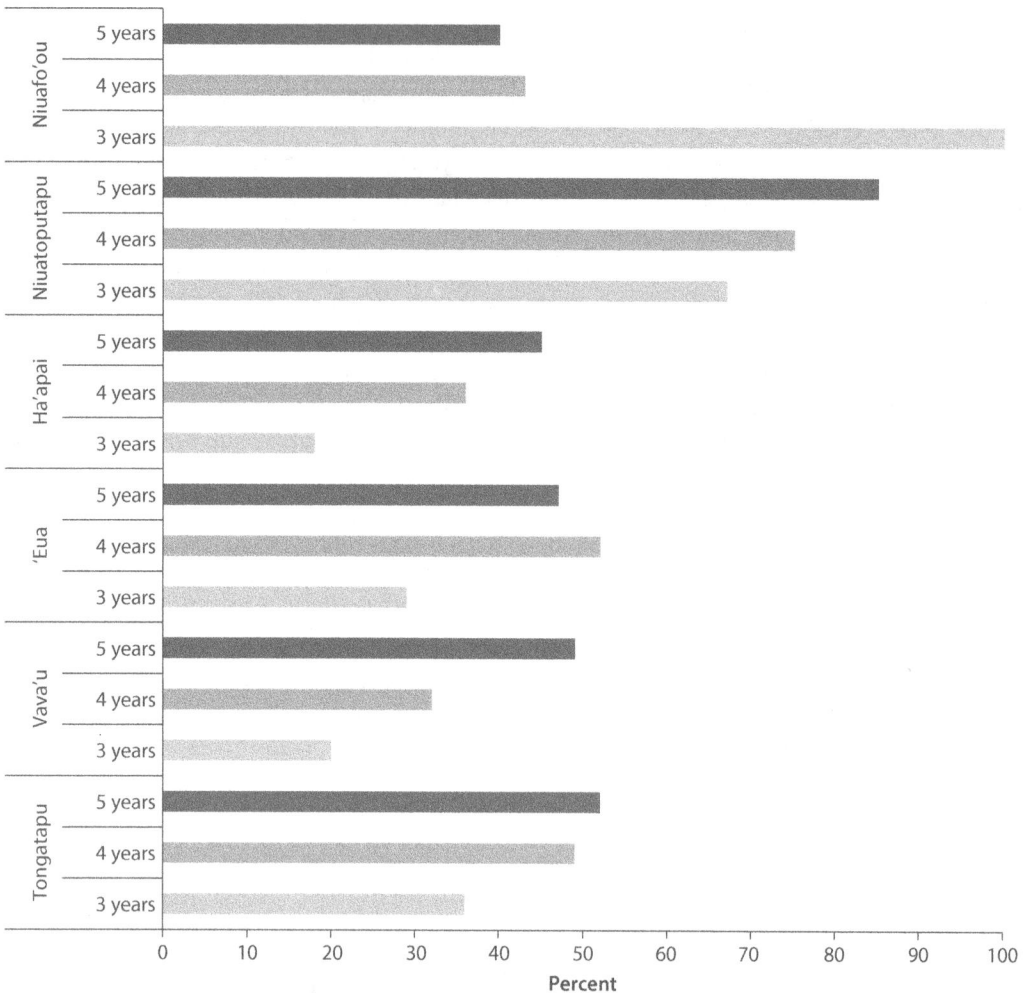

A mother's educational level is also strongly associated with her children's participation in preschool (figure 4.5). These results are consistent with global experience; namely, the more highly educated the mother, the more likely their children are to participate in education services. These results are also consistent across a child's age and gender. In Tonga, only 24 percent of children born to mothers who went to primary school participate in preschool, whereas 67 percent of children born to mothers with tertiary education participate in early education services. Taken together, these results indicate the PEARL program is both well targeted and well placed through its various pillars, including increasing parental awareness of the importance of early child development and increased opportunities for participation in community-based early education programs.

Figure 4.5 Preschool Participation by Mother's Education Level

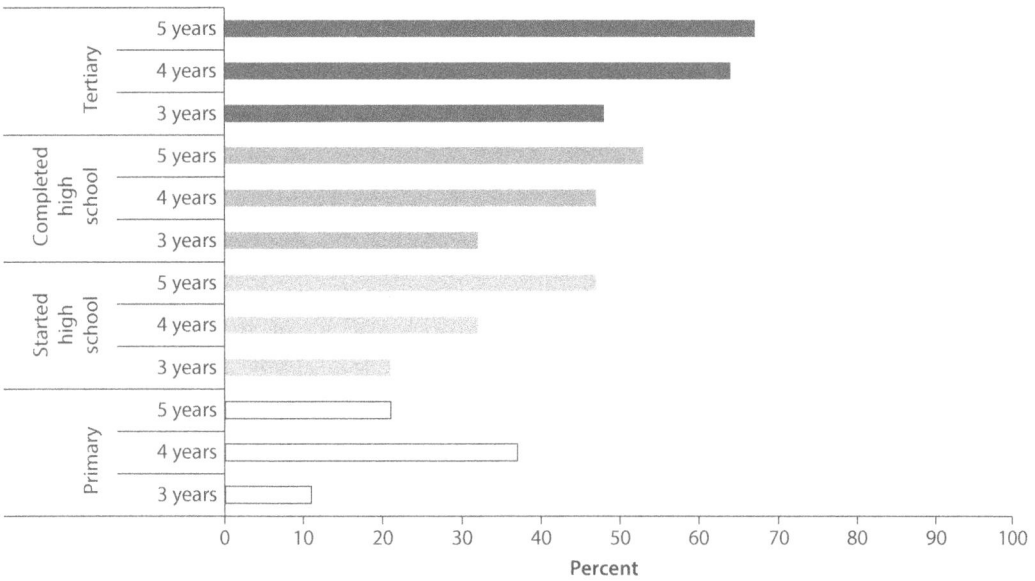

Table 4.16 Relationship between Participation in Early Childhood Education and Developmental Outcomes

Does/did this child attend kindergarten/ children's center?		Physical	Verbal	Cultural/ spiritual	Social/ emotional	Perseverance	Approaches	Numeracy/ concepts	Literacy
Yes	Mean (SD)	0.78 (0.25)	0.86 (0.21)	0.72 (0.26)	0.70 (0.21)	0.46 (0.26)	0.76 (0.30)	0.59 (0.28)	0.54 (0.30)
	N	2,792	2,798	2,784	2,786	2,801	2,797	2,775	2,780
No	Mean (SD)	0.69 (0.27)	0.84 (0.23)	0.65 (0.28)	0.64 (0.21)	0.44 (0.24)	0.68 (0.34)	0.40 (0.29)	0.35 (0.30)
	N	3,525	3,534	3,520	3,521	3,534	3,531	3,522	3,525

Note: N = number of children; SD = standard deviation.

Of most relevance here is to understand whether participation in Tonga's early childhood education services actually enhances child development, and that this impact on child development is not simply a reflection of a mother's educational level. Table 4.16 presents simple descriptive analyses showing the relationship between participation in early childhood education and developmental outcomes for each of the developmental domains captured by the TeHCI. As expected, those participating show significantly higher levels of development across all developmental domains.

This relationship was then tested using a univariate generalized linear model with the child's gender and age, and mother's education level entered as

Table 4.17 Relationship between Participation in Early Childhood Developmental Outcomes, Controlling for Confounders (N = 6,299 as a minimum)

	Physical		Verbal		Spiritual/cultural		Social/emotional	
	Mean sq	F	Mean sq	F	Mean sq	F	Mean sq	F
ECD	5.80	90.71***	0.04	0.87	2.01	29.44***	1.64	40.41***
Age	21.27	328.14***	10.70	218.40***	26.03	381.21***	11.38	280.01***
Sex	2.03	31.33***	0.58	11.88***	0.58	8.59**	0.94	23.26***
Mother's education	6.53	100.84***	1.47	30.17***	7.08	103.79***	4.45	109.53***
Early Child Development	0.00	0.05	4.90	48.85***	24.89	439.82***	21.09	338.43***
Age	8.62	142.61***	21.26	211.59***	154.32	2,726.80***	162.59	2,608.73***
Sex	1.06	17.56***	0.00	0.00	0.94	16.71***	1.44	23.13***
Mother's education	1.91	31.69***	8.00	79.67***	7.95	140.49***	8.12	130.38***

Note: ECD = early child development; F = F statistic; N = number of children.

*$p < 0.05$, **$p < 0.01$, ***$p < 0.001$.

confounders. Participation in any early childhood education service was entered into the model as a fixed effect, and each of the developmental outcomes was modeled separately. The results in table 4.17 show that even after controlling for confounders, participation in some form of early childhood education program has a statistically significant effect on every aspect of development except for verbal skills and perseverance. Not surprisingly, the magnitude of the effect of preschool was highest for literacy outcomes and numeracy and concepts, such as an understanding of heights and weights.

Geographical Mapping

The TeHCI data was aggregated by village name and then geographically mapped by the Tonga Department of Survey and Lands, which is responsible for all the geographical mapping systems in Tonga. Previous donor funding was provided to the department for the creation of tsunami evacuation plans. As such, the software and equipment required for geographical mapping, as well as the local capacity and skills required, were leveraged for the PEARL project. For the purposes of the tsunami evacuation plans, boundary polygons for villages had already been created for all Tonga's inhabited islands. This enabled the community-level results from the TeHCI to be geographically mapped to communities that were locally meaningful, having already been locally defined and geocoded.

The maps provide the results in a pictorial format that are easy to understand. Each community is provided a color on the basis of the TeHCI results. After local consultation, it was decided to present the data by "traffic lights" (despite there being no traffic lights in Tonga) to represent how well the children were developing in one community relative to other communities. The TeHCI results at a community aggregate level were simply ranked from lowest to highest. The bottom third of communities were colored red, the middle third orange, and the top third best performing communities green. The patterns of colours across the communities provided a quick indication of how the various communities were doing relative to each other. Maps were completed for each of the main island groups (see maps 4.1–4.4) with the Niuas and 'Eua mapped on one map to reduce printing costs and enable better comparison (the Niuas and 'Eua having relatively few communities to compare against). Each of the TeHCI developmental domains were mapped individually, as well as an "overall development" outcome providing a snapshot of holistic child development. Appendix B shows maps for each domain for the Tongatapu island group.

These maps have proven to be very popular among the early child care and education stakeholders in Tonga, and exemplify the value of a census approach to the monitoring of child development. Survey samples are unable to provide robust community-level data back to communities (where every child counts), and local community members are prompted to consider how the children in their community are doing compared to neighboring communities. The maps acted as a facilitator to talk to communities at a local community level about the

Map 4.1 Overall Development Map of Tongatapu

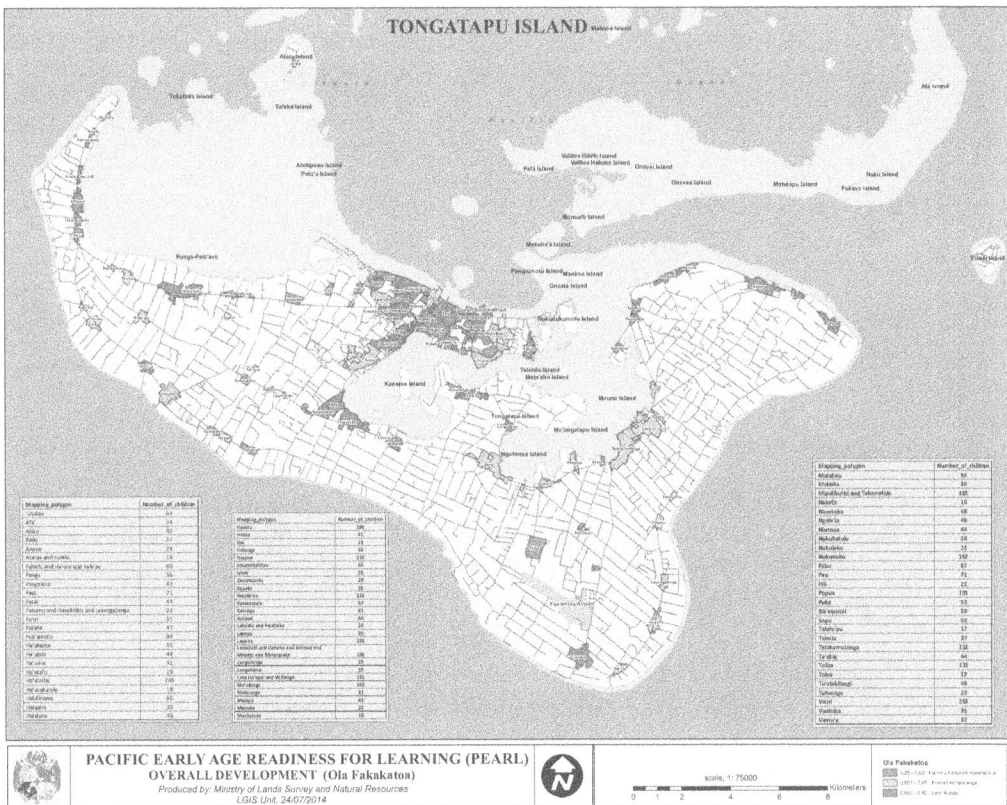

Source: Ministry of Lands, Survey and Natural Resources.

Early Childhood Development in Tonga • http://dx.doi.org/10.1596/978-1-4648-0999-6

Map 4.2 Overall Development Map of Vava'u

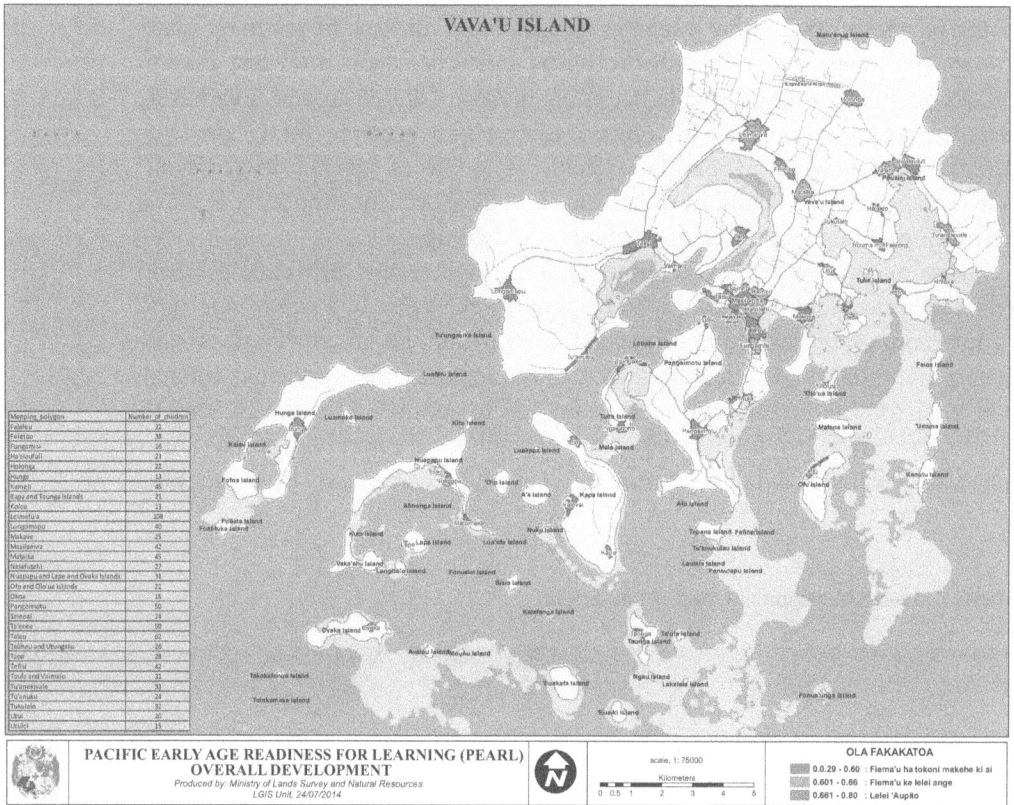

VAVA'U ISLAND

Mapping polygon	Number of children
Faletau	23
Feletoa	38
Pangaimotu	26
Ha'alaufuli	23
Holonga	22
Hunga	13
Kameli	45
Leimatu'a	11
Longomapu	108
Makave	40
Mataika	42
Matamaka	45
Ofu and Olo'ua Islands	31
Okoa	16
Pangaimotu	50
Taoa	65
Ta'anea	26
Tefisi	26
Toula	42
Tu'anekivale	31
Tu'anuku	24
Utui	20
Utulei	15

OLA FAKAKATOA

0.0.29 - 0.60 : Fiema'u ha tokoni makehe ki ai
0.601 - 0.86 : Fiema'u ke lelei ange
0.661 - 0.80 : Lelei 'Aupito

PACIFIC EARLY AGE READINESS FOR LEARNING (PEARL)
OVERALL DEVELOPMENT
Produced by: Ministry of Lands Survey and Natural Resources
LGIS Unit, 24/07/2014

scale, 1: 75000
Kilometers
0 0.5 1 2 3 4 5

Source: Ministry of Lands, Survey and Natural Resources.

importance of early childhood, while engaging and mobilizing community members around the TeHCI results in an easily understandable, locally relevant, and meaningful way. In other words, the results of *our* children in *our* community.

Data Dissemination

The TeHCI results were provided to stakeholders and communities through various avenues. Initially, the data were officially released along with the launch of the PEARL program. This was a prominent event in Tonga, with Her Royal Highness of Tonga, the Princess Salote Mafile'o Pilolevu Tuita; churches leaders; and ministerial representatives attending. Former Minister for Education Dr. 'Ana Maui Taufe'ulungaki jointly launched the results of the survey with Dr. Truman Packard, Lead Economist from the World Bank (photo 4.1). The launch was attended by representatives of all Tonga's development partners, and broadcast on local TV networks and radio programs over the following week.

Following the official release of the results, community meetings were organized to present the data to every community across Tonga. Before dissemination,

Map 4.3 Overall Development Map of Ha'apai

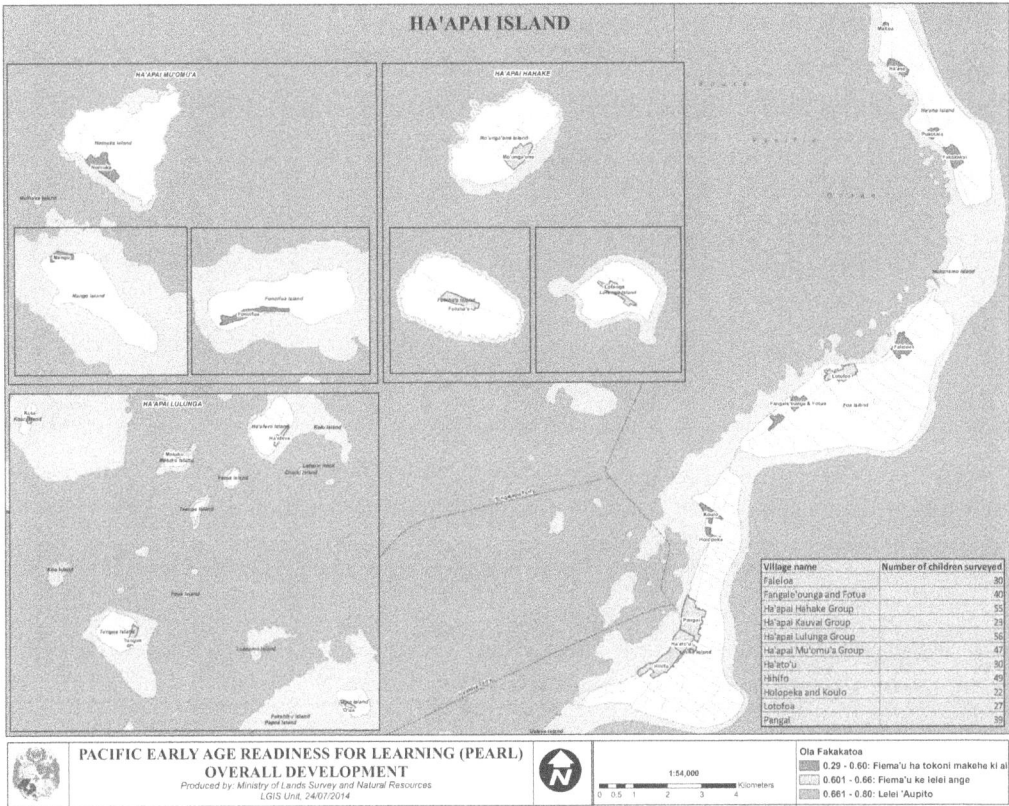

Source: Ministry of Lands, Survey and Natural Resources.

training was provided to district education officers, town officers, health person-
nel, and members of the Tonga Preschool Association in Tongatapu on communi-
cating the results presented in the maps to communities and to understand the
underlying data. They also received training on the basics of brain development
and the importance of early child stimulation to promote healthy development.
Town and district education officers went back to their island groups with
their communities' maps of child development (printed and laminated in poster
size) and training resources to disseminate the results across their communities
through town meetings (photos 4.2 and 4.3).

Further to the official launch of the results and the local community meetings,
stakeholders and policy makers were identified for personal approaches to support engagement, understanding, and their use of the data. These meetings
included the Statistics Department, Ministry of Health, Ministry of Finance, early
childhood education subsector service providers, other donor organizations, and
church leaders.

The intention is to repeat the TeHCI in 2017 as part of the evaluation of the
PEARL program. Every opportunity was taken to build local ownership, capacity,

Map 4.4 Overall Development Map of 'Eua and the Niuas

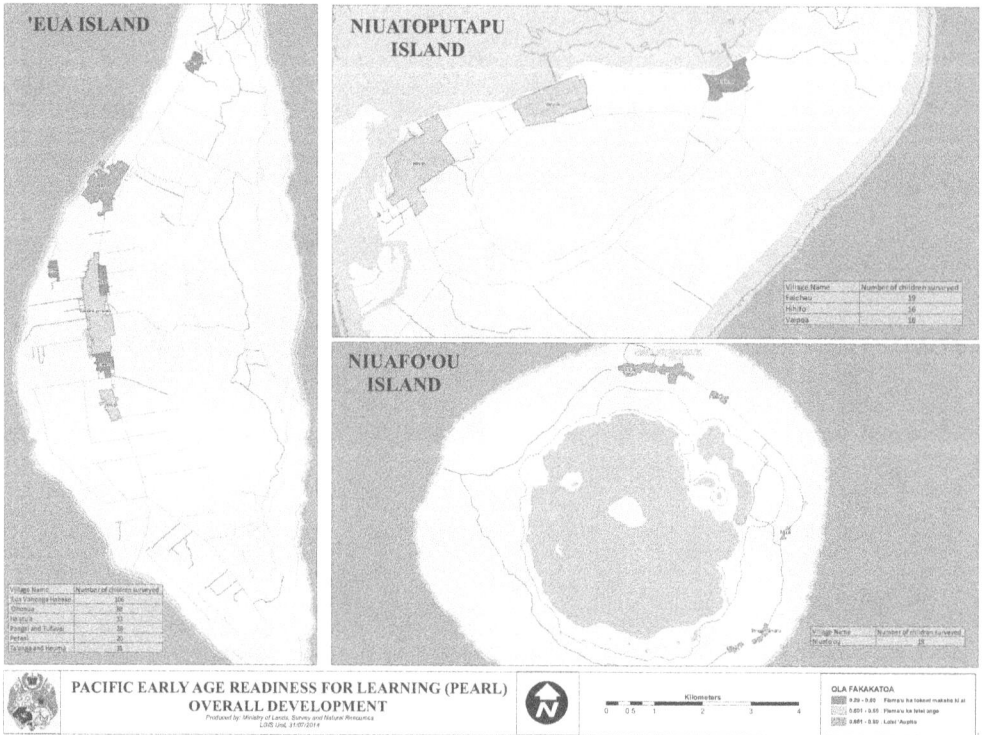

Source: Ministry of Lands, Survey and Natural Resources.

Photo 4.1 Launch of the TeHCI Results by Her Royal Highness the Princess of Tonga and Dr. Truman Packard, Lead Economist, World Bank

Source: Quang Vinh Nguyen.

Photo 4.2 Community Dissemination of the TeHCI Results on Tongatapu

Source: Sally Brinkman.

Photo 4.3 Community Dissemination of the TeHCI Results on Ui'ha Island and Ha'apai Island Group

Source: Sally Brinkman.

Early Childhood Development in Tonga • http://dx.doi.org/10.1596/978-1-4648-0999-6

and community-wide interest during the entire process of implementing the TeHCI from the original development of the instrument through to the data collection and the dissemination of results. With local teachers and community health nurses implementing the data collection, the monitoring of child development has been purposely imbedded in the system and, as far as possible, existing resources. As such, there is every hope that the government will continue the initiative after PEARL funding ceases.

CHAPTER 5

Potential Future Use of the Early Human Capability Index in Tonga and Conclusions

Exemplary Data Collection Process

The Tongan Early Human Capability Index (TeHCI) should foster understanding of the importance of early childhood development, while providing an evidence base for communities to mobilize around and for policy makers and service providers to plan around. The actual process of monitoring raises the profile of the importance of child development and, at the same time, provides a base-level of information. The process of the local creation of the TeHCI; the collection of data through local partnerships of health, education, and town officers; and widespread community level dissemination of the data should serve as a shining light and example for other countries to follow. With repeated use of the TeHCI, Tonga will be able to evaluate not only the Pacific Early Age Readiness and Learning (PEARL) Programme but also other policy changes, and changes in service delivery and community action to support early childhood development and school readiness.

Local capacities were built through the development of the TeHCI, data collection process, database, data mapping, and the dissemination of results. This included enhancing capacity in four main areas: (1) the professional development of teachers, (2) education and health systems to work together to monitor and collect population-wide data, (3) local government to analyze and geographically map the data, and (4) community awareness of the importance of early childhood development and early education. The PEARL program is building on these capacities to support the development and delivery of community-based playgroups to enhance child development and school readiness.

The goal is to build Tonga's capacity for translational science—the ability to turn the data into relevant information for communities, policy makers, and service providers. We hope the data will continue to be used and there will be an appetite to repeat the TeHCI data collection, because only with repeat data collections will communities know if their efforts to support the children in their community are reaping rewards. At a national level, with the changing early education system slowly rolling out, it will also be important to determine the impact these changes in service delivery are having on the population of Tongan children over time.

The cost of carrying out data collection and dissemination of the TeHCI in 2014, not including technical assistance from the World Bank, was about US$100,000. This included the costs of data collection, map development and printing, and disseminating the results. The Government of Tonga's travel allowance has increased since 2014, which could add about U$20,000 to the next round of the TeHCI. Technical assistance supported development of the instrument, data analysis and results reporting, and training on enumeration and dissemination, added about US$60,000 to the cost of the TeHCI in 2014. This will be reduced for the second round of the TeHCI in 2017 because there will be less work required on developing the instrument, and technical assistance in subsequent rounds should cost even less due to the local capacity building under the PEARL program. It will be worthwhile to continue to collect the data periodically to monitor the progress of implementation and to inform the government's related policy decisions. The TeHCI data could also be used as a base to determine how the different education systems, through different curriculum strategies, might be supporting children in Tonga to ensure that all of them can enjoy the same quality of education services regardless of where they live and who the service providers are. In the future, TeHCI data could be used as evidence to inform funding decisions to ensure equity and efficiency. With the single TeHCI assessment of children's development, and then following these children up over time, the government and church-led education sectors would be able to better evaluate their programs. For example, the World Bank aims to use the TeHCI data as a baseline for children who then move into the reading interventions of the PEARL program. The evaluation of PEARL's reading component is enhanced by having a broad baseline indicator of a child's development before coming into the school system, and before being exposed to the reading component.

Conclusions

It is still difficult to convince many governments about the value of investing in early child development, despite a growing body of evidence of the value of this intervention. School readiness lays the foundation for educational success and achievement. Consequently, the significance of school readiness is noted both as an intrinsic benefit in improving education outcomes for children by completing primary school, staying in high school, and productivity in adulthood. In addition, societies benefit from the human capital created through a strong foundational start. With the knowledge that both poverty and inequality are damaging conditions for child development, social policy and cultural change are required to redress the power formations, social arrangements, values, and practices that can often hold children back from their developmental potential.

A key challenge is that important issues risk invisibility in the absence of comprehensive data. A deeper understanding of the capabilities that are strengthened by interventions and the causal mechanisms that explain program impact, along with the dose and quality required is essential for confidence by policy makers to invest in early child development (Lynch and others 2010). Most early childhood research has been conducted in a relatively small number of economically affluent nations, especially the United States, leaving huge gaps in knowledge about the state of child development in marginalized and diverse communities. This unequal distribution of data collection is a major challenge for increasing global awareness of the importance of early child development in shaping future human capital.

As UNICEF noted in a report on child well-being, "Measurement serves as the hand-rail of policy, keeping efforts on track towards goals, encourages sustained attention, gives early warning signs of success or failure, fuels advocacy, ensures accountability, and helps decision making in relation to the most effective allocation of resources" (UNICEF 2007). With public access to the results of monitoring, civil servants, nongovernment organizations, aid agencies, and the media are able to advocate for children and families, promoting new policy issues to be recognized and addressed. Policy making, service planning, and community development strategies are increasingly required to be based on evidence. The extent and nature of the problems can be quantified to inform the policy actions required.

Many Western trained methodologists aim to create international measures that can reliably show differential child development across countries so that it becomes possible to investigate how cultural practices and norms may impact on child development. In other words, culture should not be part of the measured aspect of development (dependent variable), but instead be captured in the measured aspect of the independent variables. Attempts to create this equivalence may make sense when measuring basic aspects of developmental milestones, such as when a child starts to walk, but other aspects of school readiness are highly culturally loaded. For example, as noted earlier, a child in regions of Latin America is praised for being talkative, and it is considered an early indicator of intelligence if the child interrupts others to participate in conversations. The same attributes in Pacific Island countries, however, would be considered an early indicator of a disrespectful child who is slow to learn. Most Western-based indicators of school readiness attribute the same behavior somewhere in between; that is, talkativeness is considered a positive attribute, but a child who interrupts others to be talkative is considered disrespectful. Within each local culture and thus within the local preschool and school systems, these attributes are important and valid indicators of school readiness, and, so to be relevant, culture should be imbedded within the measure. It is therefore questionable whether it should even be an aim to make a single measure "equivalent," and whether equivalence would even be achievable without alienating one culture over another.

Tonga is the second country in the world to undertake a census of child development across its entire population. Australia was the first, conducting a census once every three years of children in their first year of full-time schooling. With almost the entire population of children attending school in Australia, this has been an extremely efficient method of data collection. Unlike Australia, the data capture in Tonga was for three- to five-year-olds (whereas in Australia it is a single-year cohort with most children aged five). As such, this made the data collection in Tonga more complex, because not all children are attending a single form of early childhood education or health system at any one point in time to act as a system-wide data collection point. This meant that in Tonga an innovative, mixed-method, and cross-sector partnership approach to the data collection was used. Tonga's ability to conduct a census of three- to five-year-old children through a partnership approach between health, educa-tion, and local town officers is to be commended, and should be seen as a pragmatic model for the world to consider. Tonga now has reliable, detailed, local-level data that captures the entire country. Both the data collection process in itself, as well as the dissemination of the data, is helping to raise awareness of the importance of early childhood development, and provides a platform for monitoring policies and evaluating programs such as PEARL and their impact on the children of Tonga.

Back-Translated and Tongan Versions of the TeHCI

Identificaion number _____

The Tongan Early Human Capability Index (TeHCI)

Backtranslated to English

Teacher Completed

For each question, please mark the box that represents your answer. It is important to remember that children do not develop and learn at the same rate; for example, some children learn to walk earlier than others and this is normal and OK. We don't expect children to be able to do everthing we ask in this questionnaire. The most important thing is that you give honest answers.

Your answers need to be accurate. We are trying to find out the true status of the children, so that we know how and where we can best help.

There will be some questions that you will need to work with paretns to answer.

The data is not used to judge the school or teaching strategies but to work out where children need help with their development.

The child's name won't be used for anything and the data is kept confidential.

Name of kindergarten: _____

Background information

A   Child's name   _____

B   Child's date of birth   _____ / _____ / _____

		Male	Female
C	Child's gender	◯	◯

		Primary	Started High
D	Education level of child's mother	◯	◯
		Completed High	**Tertiary**
		◯	◯

E   Community where the child lives: _____

Physical health

1   Child's height   _____ cm

2   Child's weight   _____ kg

		Yes	No
3	Is this child frequently sickly?	◯	◯
4a	Does this child have any disabilities / special needs? (or needs help with)	◯	◯
4b	If yes _____		
	_____		
5	Does this child have good hygiene; i.e., always washes his/her hands after toileting	◯	◯
6	Does this child have positive habits, mafai/fili fakapotopoto	◯	◯
7	Does this child know good foods from bad foods	◯	◯

General verbal communication

		Can already	Can't yet
8	Can this child use a group of words?	◯	◯
9	Can this child use a string of sentences?	◯	◯
10	Can this child take turns speaking in a conversation?	◯	◯
11	Can this child describe things in detail with good Tongan words?	◯	◯
12	Can this child hold an adult-like conversation (for example, talkative, always questioning)	◯	◯

Cultural identity and spirituality

	Can already	Can't yet
13 Shows compassion, understanding and tolerance of others	○	○
14 Can this child identify two culturally important foods / dishes?	○	○
15 Can this child identify two local plants that provide food / fruits?	○	○
16 Does this child show the Tongan cultural values of humility?	○	○
17 Does this child show loyalty and commitment?	○	○
18 Does this child show reciprocity in relationships	○	○
19 Does this child actively participate in cultural routines, i.e., dance?	○	○
20 Is this child able to say a short prayer?	○	○

Social and emotional well-being and skills

	Yes	No
21 Is this child happy to share his/her toys and belongings?	○	○
22 Does this child take care of his/her own things?	○	○
23 Does this child demonstrate respect for adults?	○	○
24 Does this child demonstrate respect for other children?	○	○
25 Does this child accept responsibility for his/her actions?	○	○
26 Is this child considerate of other people's feelings?	○	○
27 Does this child repeatedly do something wrong even though he/she has been told to stop	○	○
28 Is this child always helpful?	○	○
29 Is this child friendly to other children?	○	○
30 Does this child kick, bite or hit adults or other children?	○	○

	Yes	No
31 Is this child impatient?	○	○
32 Does this child always understand the difference between right and wrong?	○	○
33 Does this child follow simple directions on how to do something?	○	○

Perseverance

	Yes	No
34 Does this child always perform tasks independently?	○	○
35 Does this child always keep at a task until he/she is finished?	○	○
36 Does this child need constant reminding to finish something off?	○	○
37 Does this child get easily distracted from a task?	○	○

Approaches to learning

	Yes	No
38 Does this child show more curiosity about something new in comparison to something familiar?	○	○
39 Does this child investigate/explore the function of a new toy/game/puzzle or object?	○	○
40 Is this child always wanting to learn new things?	○	○
41 When in an unfamiliar environment with a familiar person present, does this child feel free to explore?	○	○
42 Is this child always diligent in his/her approach to a new job or task?	○	○

Numeracy and concepts

	Can already	Can't yet
43 Can this child recognize zeometric shapes (e.g., triangle, circle, square)?	○	○
44 Can this child name and identify at least 3 colours?	○	○
45 Can this child sort and classify objects by common characteristics (e.g., shape, colour, size)?	○	○
46 Can this child name and recognise the symbol of all numbers from 1 to 10?	○	○
47 Can this child count to 10?	○	○

	Yes	No
48 Can this child count to 20?	◯	◯
49 Can this child count to 100?	◯	◯
50 Does this child know that a horse is taller than a dog?	◯	◯
51 Does this child know the order of the day (e.g., morning, then afternoon and then evening)?	◯	◯
52 Does this child understand the concepts of yesterday, today and tomorrow?	◯	◯
53 Does this child know that a vehicle weighs more than a cup?	◯	◯
54 Does this child know that the number 8 is bigger than the number 2?	◯	◯

Formal literacy - reading

	Can already	Can't yet
55 Does this child know the sounds of three letters of the alphabet? (phonics)	◯	◯
56 Can this child identify at least 3 letters of the alphabet?	◯	◯
57 Can this child identify at least 10 letters of the alphabet?	◯	◯

	Yes	No
58 Are there any reading materials in the child's home (e.g., picture books, magazines)	◯	◯

	Can already	Can't yet
59 Can this child hold a book and turn the pages in the right way?	◯	◯
60 Can this child follow reading directions? (i.e., left to right, top to bottom)	◯	◯
61 Can this child read at least 4 simple popular words?	◯	◯

Formal literacy - writing

	Can already	Can't yet
62 Can this child draw something identifiable? (e.g., a stick person)	◯	◯
63 Can this child copy (trace) the shape of a letter?	◯	◯
64 Can this child write at least 3 letters? (e.g., A, B, C)	◯	◯
65 Can this child write their own name?	◯	◯
66 Can this child write simple words?	◯	◯

Identification number _____

The Tongan Early Human Capability Index (TeHCI)

Backtranslated to English

Parent Completed

For each question, please mark the box that represents your answer. It is important to remember that children do not develop and learn at the same rate; for example, some children learn to walk earlier than others and this is normal and OK. We don't expect children to be able to do everthing we ask in this questionnaire. The most important thing is that you give honest answers.

We are trying to find out the true status of the children, so that we know how and where we can best help. The survey is not to rate your parenting style but to get general information about children and for us to learn where best to help.

The child's name won't be used for anything and the data is kept confidential.

Name of fieldworker _____

Background information

A   Child's name   _____

B   Child's date of birth   _____ / _____ / _____

	Male	Female
C Child's gender	○	○

	Primary	Started High
D Education level of child's mother	○	○

	Completed High	Tertiary
	○	○

E   Community where the child lives: _____

Physical health

1   Child's height   _____ cm

2   Child's weight   _____ kg

	Yes	No
3 Is this child sickly, not well looked after?	○	○

	Yes	No
4a Does this child have any dificulties or special needs that he/she requires help with 4b If yes _____ _____	◯	◯
5 Does this child have good hygiene; i.e., always washes his/her hands after toileting?	◯	◯
6 Does this child have positive habits, mafai/fili fakapotopoto	◯	◯
7 Does this child know good foods from bad foods	◯	◯

General verbal communication

	Can already	Can't yet
8 This child use a group of words in talking?	◯	◯
9 Can this child converse with others?	◯	◯
10 Can this child talk about something that he/she has done?	◯	◯
11 Can this child give detail using good Tongan words?	◯	◯
12 Can this child hold an adult-like conversation (e.g., talkative, always questioning)	◯	◯

Cultural identity and spirituality

	Can already	Can't yet
13 Shows compassion, understanding and tolerance of others	◯	◯
14 Can this child identify two culturally important foods / dishes?	◯	◯
15 Can this child identify two local plants that provide food / fruits?	◯	◯
16 Does this child show the Tongan cultural values of humility?	◯	◯
17 Does this child show the Tongan cultural values of devotion/commitment/obligation/responsibility?	◯	◯
18 Does this child show the Tongan cultural values of reciprocity in relationships	◯	◯
19 Does this child participate in cultural routines (e.g., dance)?	◯	◯
20 Is this child able to say a short prayer?	◯	◯

Social and emotional well-being and skills

	Yes	No
21 Is this child happy to share his/her toys and belongings?	◯	◯
22 Does this child take care of his/her own things?	◯	◯
23 Does this child demonstrate respect for adults?	◯	◯
24 Does this child demonstrate respect for other children?	◯	◯
25 Does this child accept responsibility for his/her actions?	◯	◯
26 Does this child repeatedly do something wrong even though he/she has been told to stop	◯	◯
27 Is this child considerate of other people's feelings?	◯	◯
28 Is this child always helpful?	◯	◯
29 Is this child friendly to other children?	◯	◯
30 Does this child kick, bite or hit adults or other children?	◯	◯
31 Is this child impatient?	◯	◯
32 Does this child always understand the difference between acceptable and non-acceptable behaviour?	◯	◯
33 Does this child follow simple directions on how to do something?	◯	◯

Perseverance

	Yes	No
34 Does this child always perform tasks independently?	◯	◯
35 Does this child always keep at a task until he/she is finished?	◯	◯
36 Does this child need constant reminding to finish something off?	◯	◯
37 Does this child get easily distracted from a task?	◯	◯

Approaches to learning

		Yes	No
38	Does this child show more curiosity about something new in comparison to something familiar?	◯	◯
39	Does this child investigate/explore the function of a new toy/game/puzzle or object?	◯	◯
40	Is this child always wanting to learn new things?	◯	◯
41	When in an unfamiliar environment with a familiar person present, does this child feel free to explore?	◯	◯
42	Is this child always diligent in his/her approach to a new job or task?	◯	◯

Numeracy and concepts

		Can already	Can't yet
43	Can this child recognize geometric shapes (e.g., triangle, circle, square)?	◯	◯
44	Can this child name and identify at least 3 colours?	◯	◯
45	Can this child sort and classify objects by common characteristics (e.g., shape, colour, size)?	◯	◯
46	Can this child name and recognize the symbol of all numbers from 1 to 10?	◯	◯
47	Can this child count to 10?	◯	◯
48	Can this child count to 20?	◯	◯
49	Can this child count to 100?	◯	◯

		Yes	Not yet
50	Does this child know that a horse is taller than a dog?	◯	◯
51	Does this child know the order of the day (e.g., morning, then afternoon and then evening)?	◯	◯
52	Does this child understand the concepts of yesterday, today and tomorrow?	◯	◯
53	Does this child know that a vehicle weighs more than a cup?	◯	◯
54	Does this child know that the number 8 is bigger than the number 2?	◯	◯

Formal literacy - reading

	Can already	Can't yet
55 Does this child know the sounds of the alphabet? (phonics)	○	○
56 Can this child identify at least 3 letters of the alphabet?	○	○
57 Can this child identify at least 10 letters of the alphabet?	○	○

	Yes	No
58 Are there any reading materials available to the child (e.g., picture books, magazines)	○	○

	Can already	Can't yet
59 Can this child hold a book and turn the pages in the right way?	○	○
60 Can this child follow reading directions? (i.e., left to right, top to bottom)	○	○
61 Can this child read at least 4 popular words?	○	○

Formal literacy - writing

	Can already	Can't yet
62 Can this child draw something identifiable? (e.g., a stick person)	○	○
63 Can this child copy (trace) the shape of a letter? (e.g., A, E, F)	○	○
64 Can this child write his/her own name?	○	○
65 Can this child write short and simple words?	○	○
66 Can this child write short and simple sentences?	○	○

General questions

	Yes	No
67a Does/did this child attend kindergarten/children's center?	○	○
67b If yes, what year did they start kindergarten?	○	○
67c If yes, how long did they spend in kindergarten?	○	○
67d If yes, give the name of the kindy and why you sent them?	○	○

If no, why didn't they go to kindy?

_____

_____

In the past 3 days, did you or any household member over 15 years of age engage in any of the following activities with your child?

	Yes	No
68a Read books or looked at picture books with	◯	◯
68b Told stories to	◯	◯
68c Sang song to / or with	◯	◯
68d Took outside the home/yard	◯	◯
68e Played with	◯	◯
68f Named, counted or drew things to/with	◯	◯

APPENDIX B

Geographically Mapped Results of TeHCI Domains

Map B.1 Approaches to Learning, Tongatapu

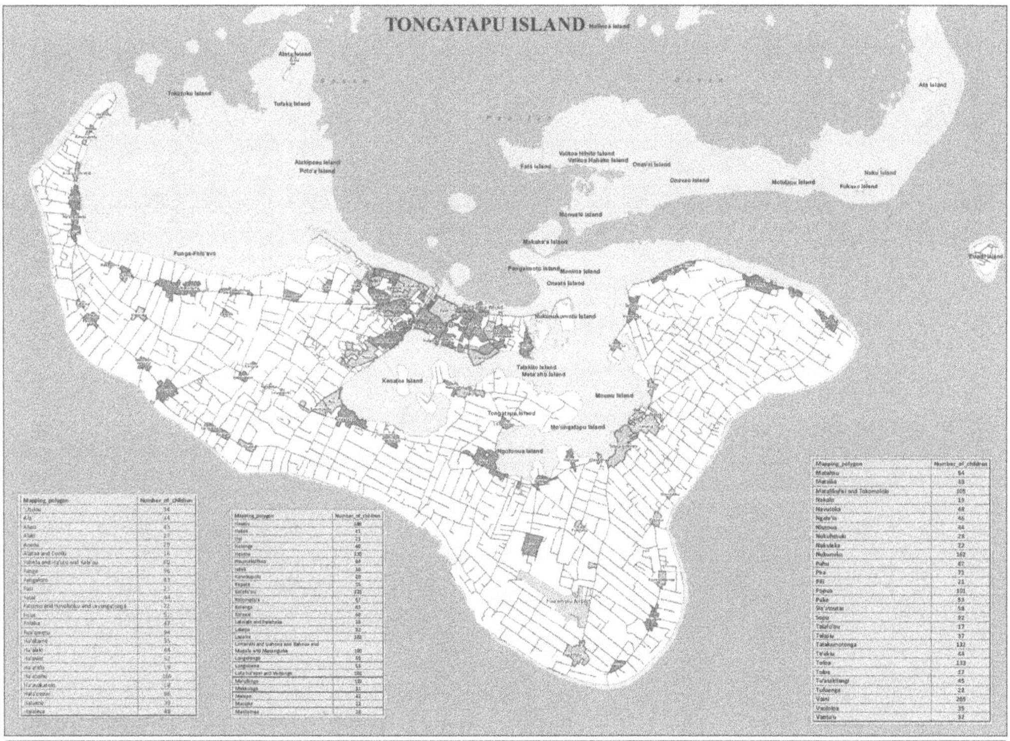

Map B.2 Cultural and Spirituality, Tongatapu

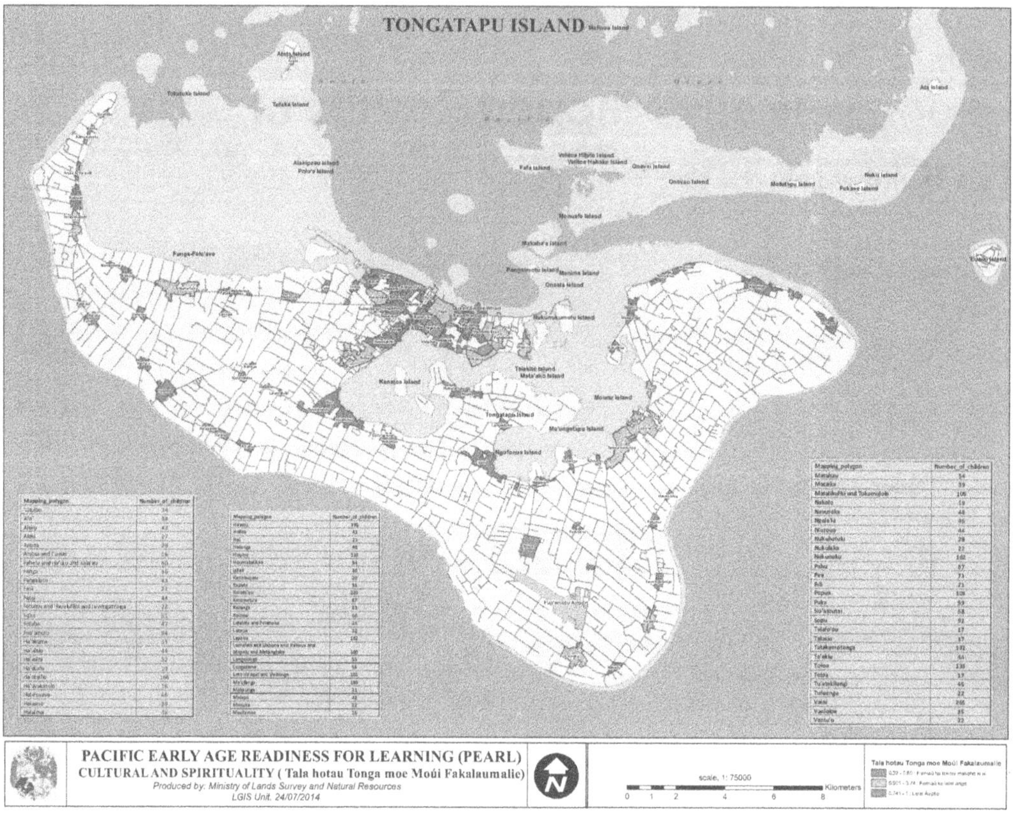

Map B.3 Literacy, Tongatapu

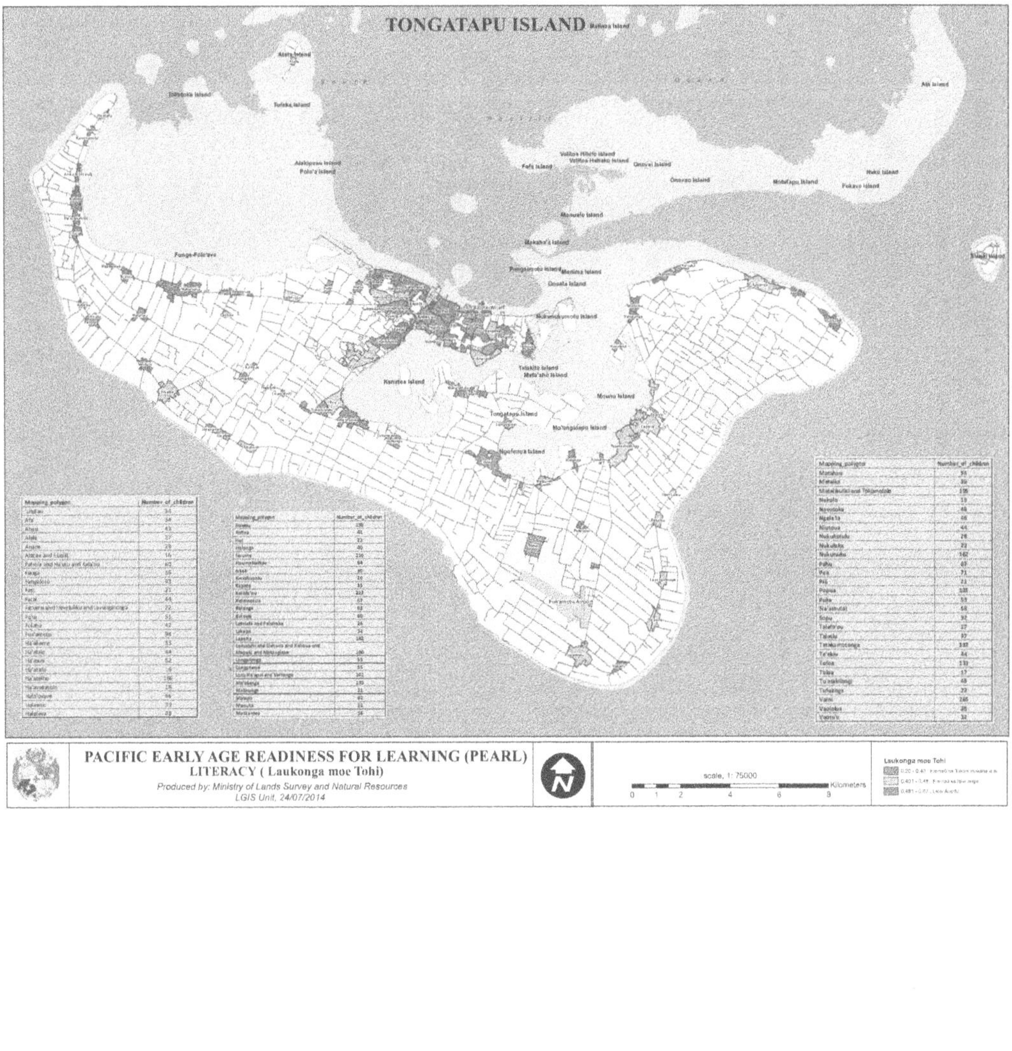

Map B.4 Numeracy and Concepts, Tongatapu

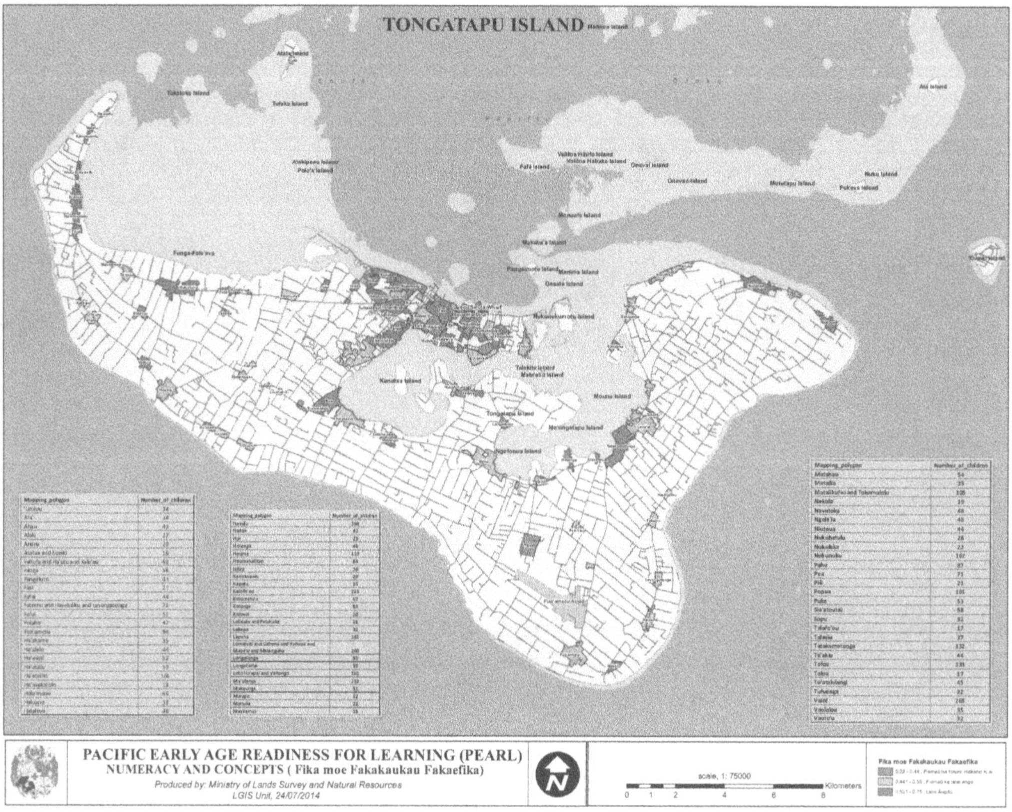

Map B.5 Perseverance, Tongatapu

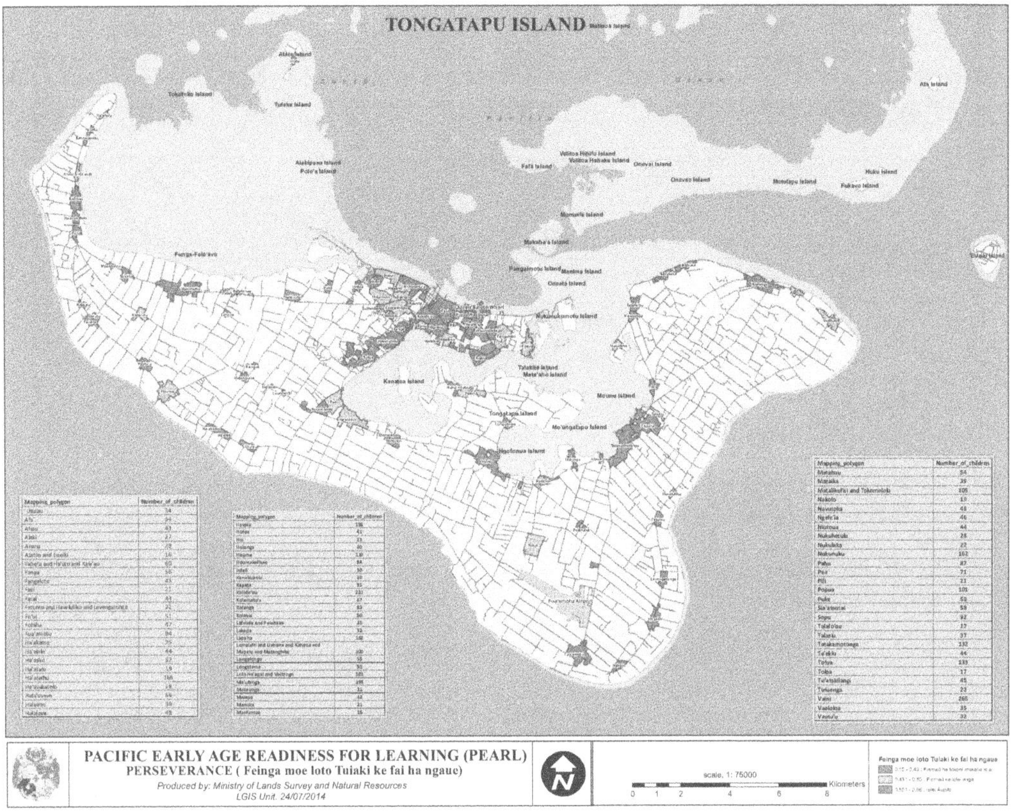

PACIFIC EARLY AGE READINESS FOR LEARNING (PEARL)
PERSEVERANCE (Feinga moe loto Tuiaki ke fai ha ngaue)
Produced by: Ministry of Lands Survey and Natural Resources
LGIS Unit. 24/07/2014

scale. 1: 75000

Early Childhood Development in Tonga • http://dx.doi.org/10.1596/978-1-4648-0999-6

Map B.6 Physical Development, Tongatapu

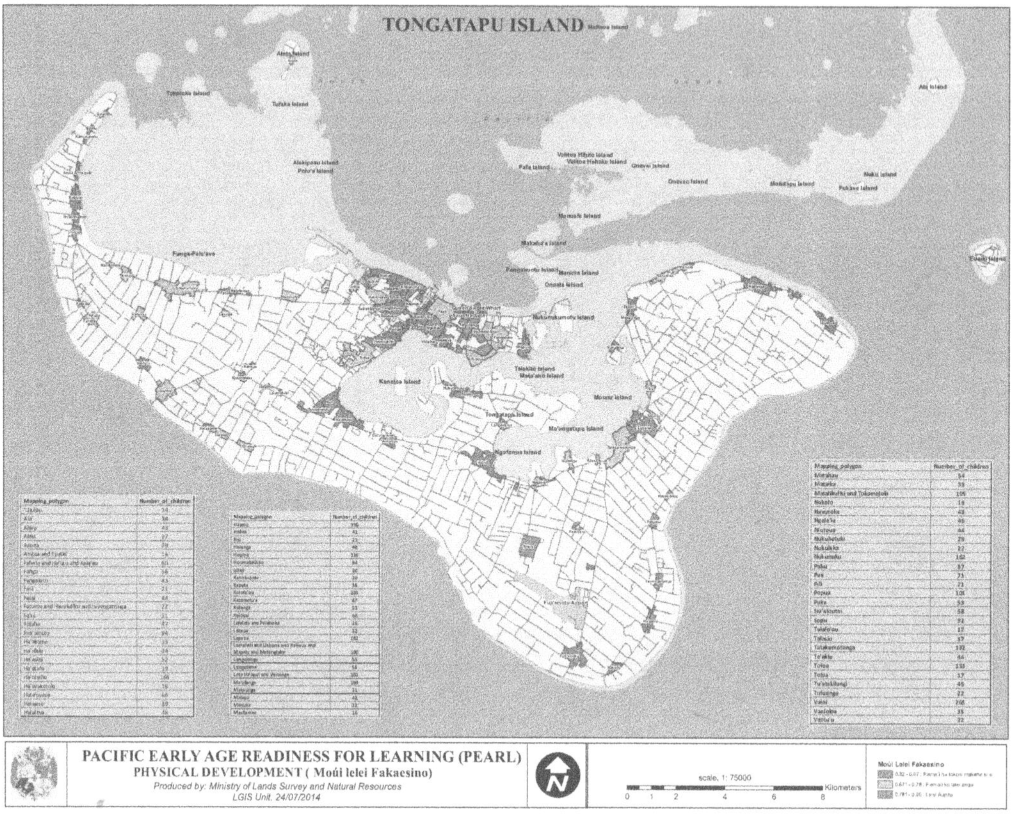

Map B.7 Social and Emotional Development, Tongatapu

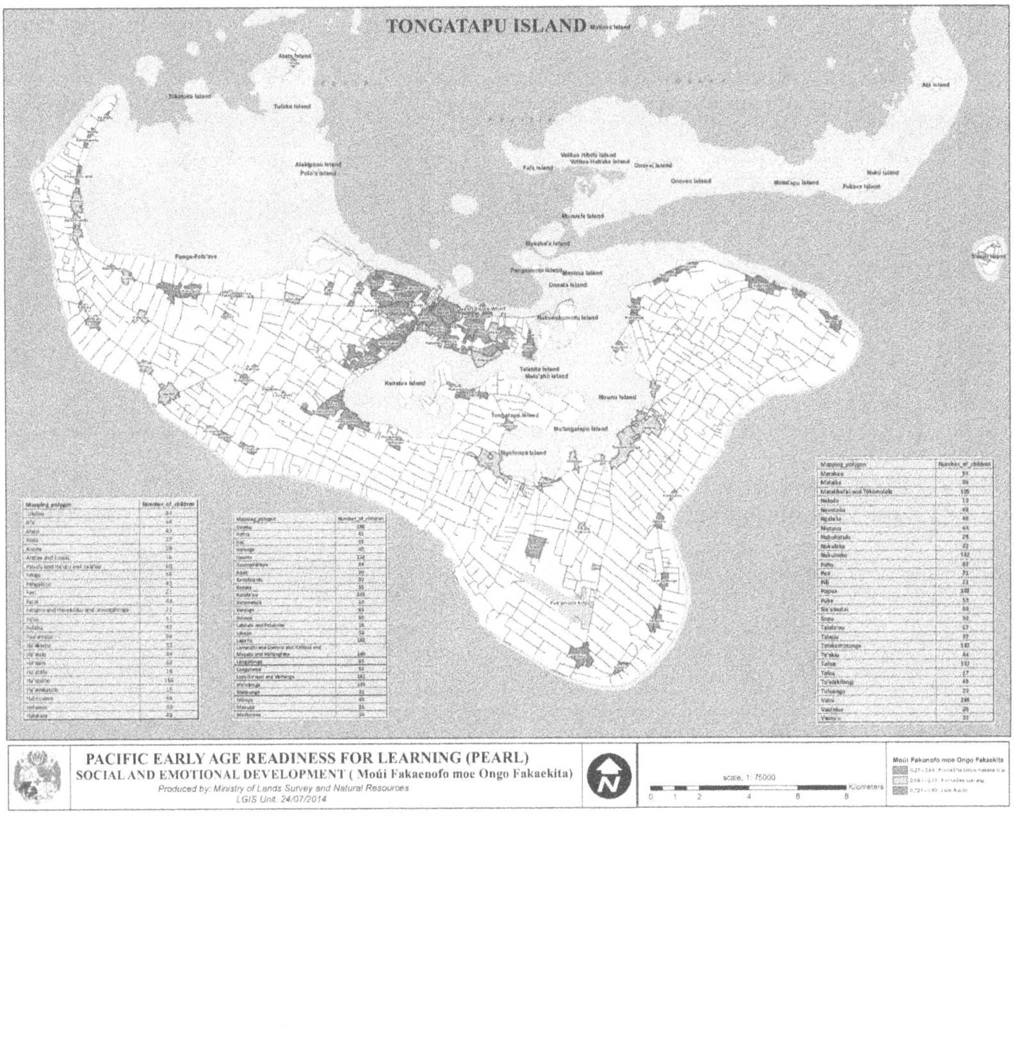

Map B.8 Verbal Development, Tongatapu

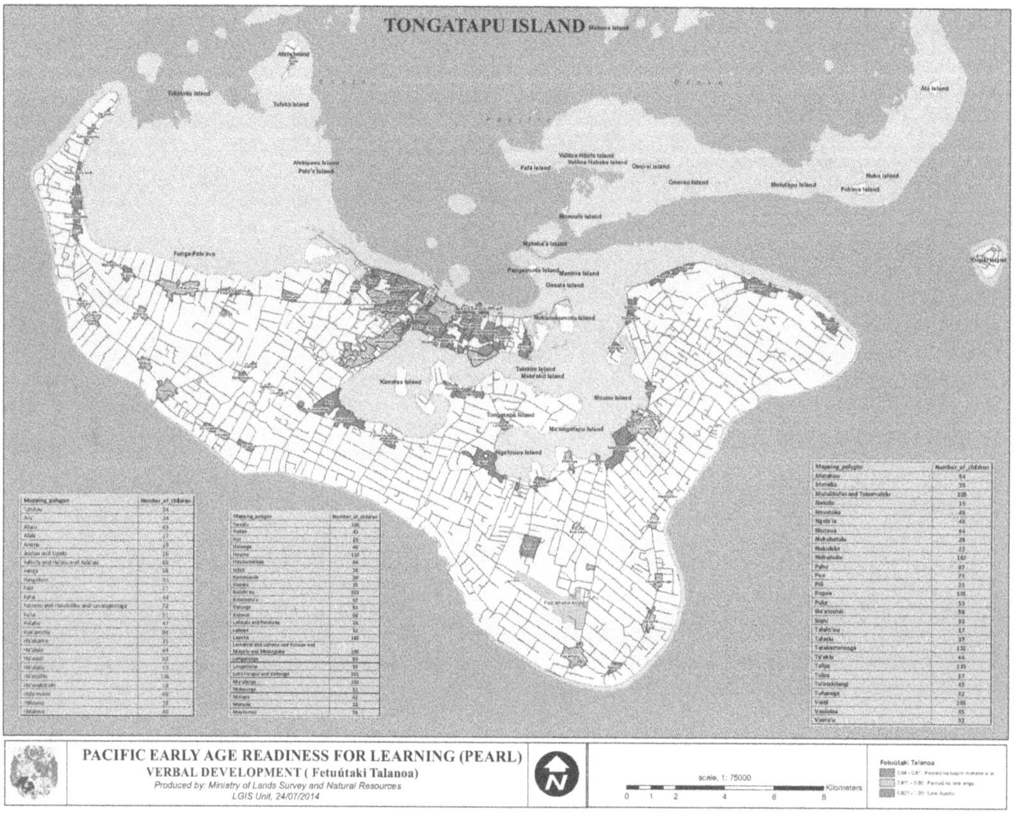

Reliability and Validity of the TeHCI

Discrimination

The results shown in chapter 4 show that the Tongan Early Human Capability Index (TeHCI) discriminates by age, gender, and mother's educational level in the expected direction and by the expected relative magnitude for each of the various domains. Hearteningly, the TeHCI is also able to differentiate differences in development by other aspects of the home environment, such as reading books at home and access to early education services before schooling. Each of these results is meaningful in its own right, but the results also imbue confidence in the instrument being sensitive to change, and being able to capture the impacts of interventions on the various domains of development.

Traditional Methods of Scale Reliability

Among traditional methods of instrument reliability, particularly in the field of psychology, is Cronbach's alpha to determine the scale fit. As a whole instrument, the TeHCI performs well with a Cronbach alpha of 0.94 (number of items 63, N = 6,348). Each domain within the TeHCI was then tested with the following results:

Overall, the results are fairly good, with most subscales/domains reaching an alpha of between 0.725 and 0.892, which is within the conventional wisdom as reaching sound reliability values. However, neither the perseverance nor the physical scale reach what would be considered a strong enough alpha value to be considered a scale in itself.

Despite these positive results, it should be noted that the use of Cronbach's alpha has been critiqued in the literature for not being an adequate test of reliability. Indeed, when it comes to the assessment of instruments, different disciplines have very different methods to determine reliability and validity. The most critical aspect of validity (that most disciplines would agree on) is the instrument's ability to predict later outcomes of importance. For the TeHCI, however, we are unable to do this at this stage, at least not until we are able to follow-up with the children already assessed by the TeHCI and perhaps capture

Table C.1 Internal Consistency of TeHCI Scales as Measured by Cronbach's Alpha

Domain	Cronbach's alpha	Number of items
All items	0.940	63
Physical	0.468	4
Verbal	0.732	5
Cultural/spiritual	0.788	8
Social/emotional	0.725	13
Perseverance	0.222	4
Approaches	0.794	5
Numbers/concepts	0.887	12
Literacy (reading/writing)	0.892	12

their later primary school performance. In the meantime, the Rasch model is probably the toughest method of assessing the instrument's scale reliability.

Rasch Modeling

The Rasch measurement model is used to establish whether sets of items are internally consistent and can provide reliable person measures on an equal-interval scale, which is invariant across subgroups of persons. The measures may represent, for example, proficiencies, attitudes, or behaviors. The model also provides evidence of any anomalies. Based on the outcomes of analyses, recommendations and suggestions for modifications to the scale or to particular items can be made.

For the analyses reported here, the software RUMM2030 (Andrich, Sheridan, and Luo 2014) was used: it incorporates a wide range of facilities for checking item and person fit, differential item functioning, reliability, targeting of items and persons, residual item correlations, subscale analysis and equating subscales, and, of course, item and person measures, known as locations. The item and person locations are mapped on a common continuum.

Independent psychometric analyses were conducted using the Rasch model on the full TeHCI census data file by Dr. Irene Styles of the Pearson Psychometric Laboratory in the Graduate School of Education at The University of Western Australia. Dr. Styles's conclusion was that, overall, the TeHCI rated "excellent" with sound psychometric properties, as evaluated using the Rasch measurement model. Dr. Styles also concluded that "especially taking into account the complex nature of the constructs being assessed, it [the TeHCI] operates remarkably well."

More specifically, the results indicated that five items did not fit the model well relative to the majority of the items: all the misfitting items are the reverse-scored items, indicating that administrators may have had difficulty with the negatively worded items. The misfitting items were: (1) Does this child get easily distracted from a task? (2) Is this child impatient? (3) Does this child need constant reminders to finish something off? (4) Does this child kick, bite, or hit adults or other children? and (5) Does this child repeatedly do something wrong

Early Childhood Development in Tonga • http://dx.doi.org/10.1596/978-1-4648-0999-6

even though he/she has been told to stop? When these five misfitting items were deleted, the Rasch analyses showed that the reduced 61-item scale fitted the model well (with a Person Separation Index of 0.93667, indicating high reliability). Thus, the instrument as a whole could be used to provide a sound measure of child development at an individual level.

In addition to the whole instrument working as a psychometrically sound instrument, the numeracy and concepts, and the literacy-related items, can be regarded as forming a strong, meaningful subscale. Although the whole TeHCI can be used together, it is the case that, at a 1 percent level of significance, 17 percent (1,148) of the sample might be better represented by a profile of two scores; that is, a single scale with the numeracy and concepts and the literacy domains combined, and all the other scales combined (social and emotional, physical, cultural and spiritual, perseverance, and approaches to learning). However, Dr. Styles felt the patterning of differential responses on the TeHCI may be due to the fact that some students were attending preschool, rather than any issue of the underlying structure of the TeHCI. According to the Rasch models parameters, other subscales exist, but were weaker psychometrically. The overall advice is to keep the TeHCI instrument as a whole when using it as a psychometrically sound measure of an individual child's improvement in child development.

Only six of the 63 items showed differential item functioning according to the administrator (that is, teacher or caregiver response), with some items showing teachers assessing children's performance higher than parents, even when the children's total scores were the same, and some showing the reverse. These results, however, did not disrupt the overall psychometric properties of the instrument.

One of the most affirmative results from the Rasch analyses was that there was no differential item functioning according to sex, thus the scale is measuring the same construct for boys and girls. For an instrument developed in the way that the TeHCI was, this result is very exciting. Many child development instruments fail the Rasch model because of differential item functioning by gender.

An additional affirmative result from the Rasch model showed that items were located along the continuum from easiest to most difficult in an order that supported expectations. That is, the verbal and cultural items tended to be the easiest, and the numeracy and concepts and the literacy (reading and writing) items the most difficult. Comparisons of mean performances for groups classified by island, sex, mother's educational level, administrator, and early child care and education were also as expected theoretically.

References

Andrich, D., B. S. Sheridan, and G. Luo. 2005. "RUMM2020: Rasch Unidimensional Measurement Models." RUMM Laboratory, Perth.

Andrich, D., and I. Styles. 2004. "Final Report on the Psychometric Analyses of the Early Development Instrument Using the Rasch Model." Technical paper commissioned for the development of the Australian Early Development Index, Murdoch University, Perth.

Bowman, B., M. Donovan, and M. Burns. 2001. *Eager to Learn: Educating our Preschoolers*. Washington, DC: National Academy Press.

Brinkman, S., and S. Blackmore. 2003. "Pilot Study Results of the Early Development Instrument: A Population Based Measure for Communities and Community Mobilisation Tool." In *Beyond the Rhetoric in Early Intervention*. Adelaide: South Australian Government.

Brinkman, S., T. Gregory, J. Harris, B. Hart, S. Blackmore, and M. Janus. 2013. "Associations between the Early Development Instrument at Age 5 and Reading and Numeracy Skills at Ages 8, 10 and 12: A Prospective Linked Data Study." *Child Indicators Research* 6 (4): 695–708.

Brinkman, S., S. Silburn, D. Lawrence, S. Goldfeld, M. Sayers, and F. Oberklaid. 2007. "Investigating the Validity of the Australian Early Development Index." *Early Education and Development* 18 (3): 427–51.

Brooks-Gunn, J., C. Rouse, and S. McLanahan. 2007. "School Readiness and the Transition to Kindergarten." In *Racial and Ethnic Gaps in School Readiness*, edited by R. C. Pianta, M J. Cox, and K. Snow, 283–306. Baltimore, MD: Paul H. Brookes.

Goldfeld, S., M. Sayers, S. Brinkman, S. Silburn, and F. Oberklaid. 2009. "The Process and Policy Challenges of Adapting and Implementing the Early Development Instrument in Australia." *Early Education and Development* 20 (6): 978–91.

Herdman, M., J. Fox-Rushby, and X. Badia. 1997. "Equivalence and the Translation and Adaptation of Health-Related Quality of Life Questionnaires." *Quality of Life Research* 6 (3): 237–47.

———. 1998. "A Model Of Equivalence in the Cultural Adaptation of Hrqol Instruments: The Universalist Approach." *Quality of Life Research* 7 (4): 323–35.

Hou, X., I. Anderson, and E. Burton-Mckenzie. 2016. "Bending the Noncommunicable Diseases, Cost Curve in the Pacific." Background paper for Pacific Possible series, World Bank, Washington, DC.

International Test Commission. 2005. "ITC Guidelines for Translating and Adapting Tests." https://www.intestcom.org/files/guideline_test_adaptation.pdf.

Janus, M., S. Brinkman, and E. Duku. 2011. "Validity and Psychometric Properties of the Early Development Instrument in Canada, Australia, United States and Jamaica." *Social Indicators Research* 103 (2): 283–97.

Janus, M., and D. Offord. 2007. "Development and Psychometric Properties of the Early Development Instrument (EDI): A Measure Of Children's School Readiness." *Canadian Journal of Behavioural Science* 39 (1): 1–22.

Lynch, J. W., C. Law, S. Brinkman, C. Chittleborough, and M. Sawyer. 2010. "Inequalities in Child Healthy Development: Some Challenges for Effective Implementation." *Social Science and Medicine* 71 (7): 1219–374.

Ministry of Finance and National Planning. 2010. *2nd National Millennium Development Goals Report for Tonga: Status and Progress between 1990–2010.* Kingdom of Tonga.

Sandraluz, L. C., A. R. Pebley, M. E. Vaiana, and E. Maggio. 2004. *Are L.A.'s Children Ready for School?* Santa Monica, CA: RAND Corporation.

UNICEF (United Nations Children's Fund). 2007. *Child Poverty in Perspective: An Overview of Child Well-Being in Rich Countries.* http://www.unicef.org/media/files /ChildPovertyReport.pdf.

United Nations. 2010. "Status of the Convention on the Rights of the Child. Report of the Secretary-General." In *United Nations General Assembly,* 65th ed. New York: United Nations.

Young, M. E. 2007. *Early Child Development: From Measurement to Action.* Washington, DC: World Bank.

Environmental Benefits Statement

The World Bank Group is committed to reducing its environmental footprint. In support of this commitment, we leverage electronic publishing options and print-on-demand technology, which is located in regional hubs worldwide. Together, these initiatives enable print runs to be lowered and shipping distances decreased, resulting in reduced paper consumption, chemical use, greenhouse gas emissions, and waste.

We follow the recommended standards for paper use set by the Green Press Initiative. The majority of our books are printed on Forest Stewardship Council (FSC)–certified paper, with nearly all containing 50–100 percent recycled content. The recycled fiber in our book paper is either unbleached or bleached using totally chlorine-free (TCF), processed chlorine–free (PCF), or enhanced elemental chlorine–free (EECF) processes.

More information about the Bank's environmental philosophy can be found at http://www.worldbank.org/corporateresponsibility.

green
press
INITIATIVE

www.ingramcontent.com/pod-product-compliance
Lightning Source LLC
Chambersburg PA
CBHW080001280326
41935CB00013B/1718